POWER
OF A THIRD KIND

POWER
OF A
THIRD KIND

The Western Attempt
to Colonize the Global Village

Hisham M. Nazer

Westport, Connecticut
London

Library of Congress Cataloging-in-Publication Data

Nazer, Hisham M., 1932–
    Power of a third kind : the Western attempt to colonize the
global village / Hisham M. Nazer.
        p.   cm.
    Includes bibliographical references (p.   ) and index.
    ISBN 0–275–96489–2 (alk. paper)
    1. Mass media—Political aspects.   2. Ideology.   3. Power (Social
sciences)   I. Title.
P95.8.N35 1999
302.23—dc21   98–47761

British Library Cataloguing in Publication Data is available.

Library of Congress Catalog Card Number: 98–47761
ISBN: 0–275–96489–2

First published in 1999

Praeger Publishers, 88 Post Road West, Westport, CT 06881
An imprint of Greenwood Publishing Group, Inc.
www.praeger.com

Printed in the United States of America

The paper used in this book complies with the
Permanent Paper Standard issued by the National
Information Standards Organization (Z39.48–1984).

10 9 8 7 6 5 4 3 2

Contents

Preface

How little it takes to ignite the flame of human imagination. Just being alive and eager to imagine alternative thoughts and conditions is all that is required. Human beings can think about and create once unimaginable things; they can think about thinking and they can even think about ways to make others think as they do. Through the miracle of language, much of this thought is simply there, open and accessible to anyone willing to reach for it. When I walk into the quiet of my study and reach out my hand, I enter the rich labyrinth of human thought from around the world and throughout history. It is that inclination to reach out and grasp the collected experience of human thought that sets human beings apart from all of Nature. Nature and the world of human-created things will always be interesting. But, for me, the most exciting dimension of our natural world occurs when human beings move from the world of things into the endless power of human thought.

During the span of my professional life, a period of thirty-eight years, the imaginative and forceful striving of the Saudi Arabian people has turned desert into city and wasteland into modern production. These changes have brought an improved quality of life to my country. More importantly, they have brought an entirely different set of challenges. Our children are being born into a different world, a world filled with a new reality. They are a part of the endless cycle of human intention, exerting power to solve problems that only create more complex challenges. Thinking creates things. Things create more complexity. Complexity creates more demand for more imaginative thought.

I want our children to face their challenges knowing that every human being is endowed with creativity—the capacity to imagine things as they are not. I want them to know that, above and beyond all their many identifications, they are human beings. They are living members of that group of creatures, who, alone on the earth, can conceive a future and imbue a present with purposive intention.

Beyond knowing and yearning to know, I want them to demand a new international discourse, a discourse in which all nations play a major role. I want them to demand a discourse based on a commitment to embrace Man *as he is.* I want them to create their own foundations for this new discourse, a foundation built on the assumption that even if a universal culture were possible, it should include the best of all cultures. I want them to urge peoples in non-Western countries to announce that they are weary of the caricature of Man concocted in the West. They need to communicate that this concept of Man is not selling because it simply is not able to conceive of Man as he is able to imagine himself. They will need to set aside Man as *he ought to be* and willingly work with anyone who wants to realize Man as *he is and Man as he could be.*

Our children will be among the first humans on the planet to live in a world that is as global perceptually and conceptually, as it is physically. They will need to be "globally smart" if they are to protect culturally derived processes of choice. They should know that "global politics" is more than the fact of all the world's states impacting one another. They must understand that the development of "global" as a conceptual fact implicates the creation of a new politics, with new sources of power, and new understandings of the acceptability of national and individual actions.

I have always felt that waiting for time to do the shredding of ethnocentric Western assumptions is a non-strategy, as lethal as it is uncertain. In my experience, time on its own favors no one, but it does give the short-term advantage to those who rise to the level of conflict first. At the end of the day, the success of non-Western countries in preserving their identities depends more on what they contribute to human civilization than what they are able to counter. To prepare themselves for the great mission, they must brace themselves for the violent turbulence that they can breeze through only with seat belts on.

Writing this book began long before the complex task of putting words on paper. My first thanks go to my wife, Amira, for being patient with me all these years, listening to my ideas, and at times, tightening the reigns on them. My children—Jawaher, Loay, Tal, Fehr, Nudd, and Modar—will be living in the world I describe in this book. I hope their generation will be better prepared than ours to meet these new challenges.

I would also like to thank Michelle LeFurge and Dennis Winters for sharing in the long arduous work through the early morning hours to arrive at the clearest possible articulation of power of a third kind. I would especially like to thank Dennis for his help over the past fifteen years in researching materials on power, media, and foreign policy. This research lent immeasurable depth to the development of the ideas in this book, as did the many wonderful hours Dennis and I spent together discussing those great thinkers and writers on mankind, happily brainstorming ideas together. Michelle deserves a special thanks for editing the manuscript, building the bibliography, chasing the footnotes . . . and fighting nicely. Without her tenacious attention to detail and scheduling we might never have put anything on paper.

I would like to extend my gratitude to those who read the manuscript and whose comments have been made a material part of this book. Special tribute is gratefully given to the Honorable Dr. Mohamad Abdu Yamani, Dr. Abdalla Masry, Mr. Michael Rice, and Mr. James R. Dunton for their immeasurable encouragement. I also wish to thank my editors at Praeger, Dr. James T. Sabin, Gillian von N. Beebe, and Julie Cullen, for their excellent work.

Finally, a gentle nod of the head to those people who wanted me to write a memoir of my life. Maybe someday, sometime. My close friends know that, for me, disparate events never held the excitement found in searching for and discovering the pattern behind events. This book is written to these close friends, recognizing them for filling our discussions with new ideas and new perspectives on old ideas.

The readers of this book, whether they accept what it has to offer or not, also deserve my gratitude. I would hope that they take it for what it is, a continuation of a lifelong dialogue that must never end.

Introduction

Ultimately, all writing is biography. No matter how much distance a writer seeks to create, every sentence carries the weight of his life and his thoughts. My own thinking has been shaped by the experiences and ruminations of a life occurring within the boundaries of a specific time and place. Throughout these journeys of thought, I found myself revisiting the primal terrain of one human being trying to impose his vision on other human beings. To me, this is the site of human power, a terrain as charged with intention as it is with the unpredictable complexity it creates. This discussion of human power is an interrogation of the way men interpret, shape, and manipulate the way other people make sense of their world. Because this analysis begins in human subjectivity, it cannot be a simple treatise on political theory, nor a pundit's perspective on global foreign policy. It is a particular and personal analysis filled with the desire, against all odds, to begin a global discourse able to make this suddenly non-insular world just a little more comprehensible.

The concepts on human power presented here were developed from over forty years of reading, thinking, and sharing insights with similarly inclined people from all over the world. From my earliest adult days, my internal discourse was focused on Man as a political being. Human power was my first preoccupation. This focus was reflected in every day of my work. In particular, I have spent much of my internal dialogue sorting through the complexities of four dynamic concepts: human power, change, institutions, and ethnocentrism.

Like all journeys, there are stopping places, plateaus, or simply unforgettable sites where an alteration in a thought's evolution becomes indelibly fixed. One such memorable moment occurred when I was a master's degree student at University of California at Los Angeles (UCLA) in the late 1950s. When asked to rank a list of countries from most to least powerful, I argued that Egypt was the most powerful and the United States the least powerful. How could I possibly defend such a ranking?

I argued that as power expands in all its awesome inequity relative to the entities around it, the incessant demands for maintaining that level of power increase exponentially. Thus, to a certain extent and at certain historic moments, power is inversely proportional to the national interest: the more the national interest and its parameters are expanded, the more difficult it is to achieve that national interest. Why? Because of counterpower. The exertion of power to realize expanded parameters of national interest creates ever increasing demands for more use of power. With every new exertion, new vulnerabilities are realized and new resources demanded. In these terms, then, I argued that the former Soviet Union and the United States became the least powerful nations on that list because they defined national interest diametrically opposed to each other, thereby neutralizing each other. Their efforts to impose contrary world visions consumed significant resources and energies in a battle that seemed an unending struggle. By comparison, Egypt's national interest at that time was limited to ridding itself of foreign domination and gaining control of the Suez Canal. And it was able to achieve both.

My fellow students listened in disbelief and dismay. But it was my professor, Dr. Marvik, who became excited about the idea. He broke their silence and led us all into an intellectual journey deep into the labyrinth of human power. Before I took the first step, however, I was convinced that the Western view of power was mostly misplaced. Defining power as something one "has" leads only to confusion about both power and man. While one can and must "have" resources, knowledge, and the instruments needed to exert power, my own life convinced me that the imaginative, interpretative, and strategy-forming capabilities of human subjectivity are the decisive factors. This was the beginning of a personal search for Man not as he ought to be or might be, but Man *as he is*.

Power is within Man, an almost glandular force secreting Man's purposive human striving. Every thought in this book finds its source in a single premise: knowing Man demands an intimate knowledge of the process by which subjective human power flows and seeps into the crevices of Man's determination to build order and maintain permanence. This is the unique dynamic behind all human creation, the force filled with human imagination and intention incarnate in implemented subjective power. I respect and admire the way it forces cracks in the human edifice, creating ever widening spaces that mock Man's efforts to control change, openings that let in the light of a new, ever more human future.

Without going into grand theories of human ontology and evolution, I find there are three phases of human power experienced since Man's first moments of self-consciousness. First, Man sought shelter and sustenance from Nature. The best defense from storms and wild animals was found within Nature; that is, Man ran into caves or climbed trees. In the second phase of human power, Man began to understand the potential of consciousness. He could fabricate human defenses by unlocking and altering Nature, itself. Even in this second phase, however, Man was still like Nature, locked into a present time and space, unable to communicate outside of his own moment in time and his own physical place.

We do not just exist in this world; we can create our own world. Being human affords a vitally unique dimension that sets us apart from all other creatures of Nature. We have the ability to occupy and manipulate mental space. Unlike our fellow creatures, we can lift time and space and objects and other creatures into the manipulable terrain of our own thought and our own imaginations. With this human realization of the power of consciousness came the source of technology, institution-building, and our "global vision."

We are now in the foothills of a new age. During the first two phases of human power, and with increasing fluidity and dexterity, Man could wander in the limitless and spaceless terrain of imagination. But, his interactions with his fellow Man were still space bound, demanding the physical presence of at least two human beings. No matter how awesome it is to travel across the globe at mach speeds in hours, a human being still needs to "be there." The discovery of electronic communications completed the legacy begun with the discovery of writing. The handcuffs of time and space were broken when sight and sound were captured and projected without any need for Man's physical presence.

Today, Man has turned the corner from simply using the unique power of consciousness to simulating that power within technological creations. We are well on the way to realizing the world Marshall McLuhan described over three decades ago. It is a world driven by our capacity to simulate human consciousness. Through technological extensions of the abilities of that consciousness, human power *within* Man was suddenly *outside* him, imbued in a technology able to compound and reflect human consciousness.

The consciousness of people in the age of the Internet and global communications has become a human project, a target for those who wish to impose a universal vision on a totally penetrated, utterly non-insular world. The central thrust of this, the third phase in the realization of human power, will be the growing capacity of Man to enter the subjectivity of other human beings through the use of technology and the projection of mobilized meaning through symbols and images. As this technological expansion goes forward and the human systems for using it become more sophisticated, a power will be realized that will, in time, transcend military and economic leverage.

The nature of this emerging power is a more elusive phenomenon. My early thinking about power, change, institutionalization, and ethnocentrism contributed to an understanding of the political exertion of power in this third phase. Despite all the discourse about television, the "Web," and the Internet, we are only in the foothills of our ability to see the shape and meaning of these technological wonders in terms of their awesome political reach. While it is too early for anything but exploratory statements, to wait until all the evidence is in would be too late for reflective action.

Two historic facts, however, make preliminary exploration possible: first, electronic access occurs at a time when it is controlled by only a few nations; and second, these same nations enjoy de facto control of international political institutions, unchallenged military power, and unassailable advantage in the creation of new technology. Because of this concentration of physical and technological alternatives and because these nations have already begun embryonic attempts to use their advantage, early explorations of this power are possible.

Recognizing that Man has passed into the third phase of human power, this analysis will explore the political implications deriving from the use of simulations of consciousness. Let us call it *power of a third kind*. In this context, then, and because the West is the first to use it, power of a third kind refers to the historic ability of the West to use its exceptional advantages in global electronic communication systems, as well as its military, economic, and institutional leverage, to establish their political processes and assumptions as universal, culturally transcendent frameworks.

With power of a third kind, the West hopes to limit counterpower to such an extent that major Western nations will be seen by non-Western countries as deserving exceptionality from the constraints placed on other nations' actions.

At precisely this point, two roads of thought presented themselves to me. I could get deeply involved in the technological wonders themselves. This is an attractive and, I am told by friends, a thoroughly fulfilling intellectual challenge. However, my own predilections drew me down another road. This is a time of intense creativity and I wanted to explore the question of who will be the main players and how they will choose to exert this power in pursuit of expanded national interest.

Any truly sophisticated understanding of this emerging new power requires an understanding of Western culture in general. More importantly, however, it requires a new awareness of the role of intellectuals in the creation of Western thought and in the resonation of that thought in institutions and the media. In Western and in some non-Western societies, there is a rich tradition of intellectuals as people who shape and define our world and push a new understanding of ourselves. As I worked to meet the challenge of planning Saudi Arabia's development, many Western intellectuals were working with me as experts in different fields. I quickly realized that Western technological success had been gained at the loss of an intellectually meaningful concept of Man and his unique imaginative power. I came to understand that scientific inquiry had tied itself to technology, and learning was narrowed to knowledge derived from scientific empiricism. In this process, Western intellectuals not only excluded spiritual, metaphysical, and speculative knowledge from true knowledge, they became committed to the assumption that if cultures did not get rid of such unempirical thought, they were "primitive" and "backward." This distortion is with us to this day, with some intellectuals in the West still not really believing that "traditional" societies can maintain their "restrictive" assumptions while they use, much less create, technology derived from scientific method.

Actually, it seemed to me then, as it does now, that the success of scientism in creating and producing technology—a record of miraculous achievement for over three hundred years—undermined the good sense of intellectuals who simply bought the assumptions of science and applied them to Man. As a result, the West chose to see and to study human beings as though they were—like Nature—redundant, predictable, and reducible to finite materiality.

This was, I think, the beginning of the confounding of Western thought. Thought in social, economic, and political arenas was confined by the same technical use-values criteria. Intellectuals patched the fledgling promise of scientism to a number of ethnocentric constructs supposedly inherent to human existence. Then they began to attack any construct that blocked men from realizing liberal individualism and its list of "inherent" rights. By so doing, Man's power of free-wheeling imaginative knowing, his assumption that political process was derived from his own indigenous culture, and the sense that each man participates in the creation of his own history was simply lifted out of the hands and minds of human beings.

Not all Western intellectuals sited power outside of human subjectivity. One writer for whom I feel a great affinity is Herbert Rosinski. He is one of a few Western thinkers who seems to have caught the incredible excitement of power as a dynamic human fact. In his book, *Power and Human Destiny*, he writes:

Man is above all a creator, and must struggle to bring into being those things upon which he has set his heart and for which he is ready to shed his heart's blood. It is this passionate character of the struggle that gives those few energies that actually win through their unique significance as bits of reality. Each bit of reality represents a force that has come to fulfillment, something that has shown itself to be truly power by having asserted its capability of being. . . . [T]his may most appropriately be described as active or "subjective" power.[1]

Because, for me, power cannot be trapped in resources or technology, I found the Western intellectuals' perspective on human potential to be especially erroneous and a serious impediment to any effort to confront change. Working with Western consultants, I learned that they linked their concept of Man, their concept of power, and their concept of change into a chain of self-serving assumptions. The way they did it, however, locked them into the assumption that change could only happen under certain conditions and within timelines born of an entirely Western experience.

Thus, when it came to evaluating Saudi Arabia's development program, they linked technology to Western political and cultural constructs in such a way that they were blinded to the incredible potential of human power. By that time, we had come to understand how this distorted image of human power blocked a clear understanding of social and economic development in non-Western countries. Western pundits, lacking experience in non-Western cultures, demonstrated this blindness. They failed to grasp how the East and West differ with regard to constructs and how these constructs guide human lives and, in fact, human discourse. In today's technologically charged political context, placing power outside human beings allows the Western intellectual to "logically" constrict the world's richly divergent political processes to fit the narrow self-interest of a few Western nations. In effect, putting power into resources puts all the power into Western hands. Having come to understand the Western concept of Man, power, and change, I realized that I needed to expand my own theory of change to include my previous thinking on power and counterpower as subjective and intersubjective realities.

In a 1985 speech to the Chemical Manufacturers' Association in the United States, I said, "The only way to confront change is to invest in it." It was my first public statement of how subjective power is related to change and how important the genius of individual creation was to dealing with change, on its own terms, regardless of one's resources. One need not follow or imitate the Western experience to effect change, but one does need to invent one's own experience and future. What I argued in that speech was, in essence, that anyone who comes to respect change comes to know that change always wins. Those who desire to prevent change can spend talent and money denying it, clinging to a comfortable state of affairs, taking every shortcut imaginable. Yet, after all that effort, they will turn around and find the change they feared is now an established fact and, with so much time wasted, it appears much more fearsome. They now face the counterpower of increased incompetence.

In the projection of power of a third kind, then, intellectuals are the vital center of institutions and the media. The institutions are the virtual sites for establishing world consensus. Western intellectuals are in charge of writing this consensus and, in the end, validating its application in specific situations. In the media, intellectuals turn from writing and stating the institutional consensus to articulating institutional assumptions in television news and dramatic programming. Intellectuals, having traveled far from their quiet laboratories, now play a major role in the creation of global consensus and in the way all events are described for the global viewer. All of this is done entirely in Western terms.

My own thinking on power, change, institutionalization, and ethnocentrism was quickened by the awesome spread of electronic communications and the power systems forming around them. I returned to my earlier thoughts, seeking a more complete concept of power. I became convinced that, in terms of the degree of potential counterpower, the smaller, weaker nations can become stronger. Then I had a breakthrough realization. For the weaker entity, the greatest counterpower sometimes lies not in the exertion of power but in inaction itself, or in the prevention of action on the part of others. For those weaker entities who do strive to develop more equitable power positions, the area of greatest opportunity can be found in the vulnerabilities of the powerful. It is between the demand for exceptionality and the effort spent to justify it, that the need for ever wider maneuverability arises. This is where the human subjectivity of weaker nations can find a wide horizon of imaginative alternatives.

Roughly stated, the more powerful the nation, the more need for exceptionality. To justify higher levels of exceptionality, powerful nations need ever greater maneuverability. The more maneuverability needed, the more exceptionality for action is required. The more exceptionality demanded, the more actions must be seen as neutral and altruistic. The more that actions must be proven neutral and altruistic, the more constrained the powerful nation is in its transnational actions.

This marked the maturation of the early thoughts on counterpower I had in my graduate classes at UCLA. In observing nations throughout the world, I came to understand that any exertion of power creates counterpower, even by the smallest state. But, power exerted by the most powerful nations is curvilinear in terms of effectiveness and vertical in terms of resultant counterpower.

With this understanding of power and counterpower, the facade of Western projections of global reality began to crumble. Today, the primary source of counterpower for the West is its political determination to cling to intellectualized assumptions already showing significant wear and tear before the end of World War II. During the Cold War, the promotion of modernization and stages of growth was the Western mantra for human development. The zeal with which they were promoted, however, pales in significance when compared to today's intense political investment in terms like "democracy," "market democracy," and "human rights."

I also find it inaccurate when Western political writers mark the current transition as "post–Cold War" when the emerging narrative of change is from an insular to a non-insular world. If one assumes that the true watershed of these past decades is loss of insularity, not the ending of a "war," then the perspective of change directly includes the entire world. This enables all nations to work with the real problem. However, if these historic changes in our world can be defined as democracy's victory over socialism, then the assumption that we are at "the end of history" limits our discourse on change to how and when all nations can be brought into line behind a single culture and its political system.

It was natural and expected that ethnocentrism and institutions would become resources for shaping such an order. Both constructs are in full force today, offering thriving vehicles for power. In the West, ethnocentrism has moved away from its previous perception as a process signaling backwardness and hardheaded resistance to human growth and development. Today, the ethnocentrism of a few Western countries is presented as neutral and necessary for Man to realize his true nature and potential. Conversely, the ethnocentrism of the less fortunate is seen as a stubborn commitment to the past that can lead only to ethnic violence and undesirable global turbulence.

The United Nations is the best example of an institution that reflects both the specific national goals of those that control it and the values of the legions of bureaucrats who work within it. Today, its stated objectives and justifications for action and funding are monolithic mirrors of Western ideological positions. This is not limited to the United Nations alone. Nearly all human institutions begin as answers to problems and end as ways of meeting the needs of those involved in their creation and maintenance.

All of these transparent efforts toward establishing Western exceptionality signal the beginning of something new. We are witnessing an attempt to impose Western political process on all nations. Power, change, ethnocentrism, and institutionalization have been brought together in a global campaign to universalize Western culture. The liberal democratic process is presented as a global imperative on the assumption that *cultural process* and *political process* are somehow separate and discontinuous human concepts. Bureaucratized Western intellectuals are working hard to convince world leaders to share their assumption of the veracity of liberal individualism. The argument is that every human being should want to assume liberal individualism, its democratic process, and the arbitrary division of knowledge into "true reason" and eccentric speculation.

The assumptive character of Western culture requires that all nations separate culture from politics and subjective human choice from its fullest expression. Because the West sees its culture as fundamental to being human, the question of separating politics from their culture does not arise. Political process and political choice are presented to non-Western countries as entirely elective matters not related to the indigenous culture of individual nations. With this working assumption, the West sees no contradiction in praising the integrity of cultures while, in the same breath, condemning or excluding countries that are "not democratic enough" to fit their culture-specific, liberal democratic criteria. When a culturally defined, Western political system becomes the baseline for defining what is politically appropriate for all nations, culture is moved completely outside of political decision making. Then, when political conflict does arise in non-Western societies, culture becomes the ready scapegoat.

We should not assume that Samuel P. Huntington's "clash of civilizations" is inevitable. The danger lies not in the potential for confrontation, but in the framing of international discourse that excludes criticism. When culture is separated from politics, the threat of a clash of cultures becomes a way for Western countries to frame their political objectives in a neutral, "scientific" way. It is the assumption that a nation's culture can be considered separate from its political system that allows Western nations to assume that liberal democracy should be adopted by all nations, *regardless of culture*. The entire process of separating politics from culture is the Western nations' attempt to shape international discourse to exclude conflict over culture. However, the irony is that their efforts to make political systems culture-neutral can only aggravate political and cultural clashes between and within nations.

Consider the effect this will have on those non-Western nations that seem to have accepted this facile separation of politics from culture. Struggling for acceptance within this Western cultural baseline, countries outside the West have been quite willing to accept the various labels that define their place: their name, "Third World"; their grade, "developing countries"; and their frame of mind, "non-aligned nations." With their labor and their labels they strive to join the "Club of the Exceptionals," with the Group of Eight (G8) leading industrial nations checking membership cards at the door. After years of striving for acceptance within Western frameworks, these countries are still left outside, even when they have joined a club where the original founders only visit on rare occasions. Yet, the creators of the Club are loath to relinquish hard-won privileges to new members demanding equal access and open communication over problems of resources and use of facilities. Over 180 not-yet-developed-enough countries watch as this same board of directors meets and makes decisions in smaller clubs. This is hardly a club of equals for a simple ethnocentric reason: Outsiders are perceived as lacking a clear demonstration of an affinity to Western politics as the only inherently human culture.

The "Third World" of Europe—Spain, Greece, and Portugal—passed through this process when they joined the European Community. North African countries will face a more arduous road when they apply to the European Community. The real identity that grants them even the possibility of admission is that they are French or English speaking or a member of the Commonwealth—but nothing African. Now, North Atlantic Treaty Organization (NATO) membership fills the headlines and colors the dreams of Eastern European nations, a club where the conditions for inclusion are equally arbitrary and ethnocentric.

Separating politics from culture is a Western strategy for maintaining exceptionality that certainly will create counterpower of significant proportions. Because the West has chosen to trivialize culture, politics, human power, and change, the entire human process has been distorted. Western success, however, is not assured. They face incredible difficulty in establishing Western thought as universally global and inherently human unless, of course, the non-Western nations' response is totally passive. Western political strategy has one foot on the ledge of control over technology while the other reaches for a foothold on the sandstone of shaky "universal" concepts. The Western nations are pushed by their nightmares and pulled by their dreams. They fear losing their position as the most affluent consuming nations on earth at the moment when they find themselves fading as the world's leading manufacturers. Meanwhile, the Western nations are still pulled by their dream to be the unchallenged world leaders, role models of freedom and consumption.

Yet the difficulty faced by the West in its scramble to maintain exceptionality should be of little comfort to those non-Western countries that spend their time queuing up for acceptance into the "Club," while during the lunch break they regale each other with tales of the executive board's decline. Long before this decline is realized, however, the Western desperation to turn adversity into economic and political opportunity will be fraught with danger for non-Western nations. It has often been said, "When the West sneezes, the 'Rest' catch a cold." The character of the current nightmare/dream scenario of the West means that, as the international political and economic bridge is being made of reconstructed Cold War scrap, a slip for the G8 partner countries will be a free fall for the non-Western nations.

Non-Western intellectuals have an urgent need to make this erratic attempt at global ascendancy as transparently intelligible as possible. They must grasp these winds of international change with the clearest and most accurate prediction of its timing, character, shape, and impact. They must begin with the knowledge that the world is in the third phase where human creations have made this planet an ever more human world, a world where Nature's survival is nearly as dependent on us as we are on Nature. But that power also represents another realization: With the recent discovery and use of electronic communications as an extension of consciousness, Man now has unprecedented opportunities for controlling the uses of consciousness by other human beings. In fact, the question facing non-Western intellectuals is as simple as it is awesome: Is it now possible to colonize global perception? Still in a primitive stage, both technologically and in the human capacity to use it, electronic communications already shows significant promise in its ability to directly affect the way people use their imaginative and interpretative powers. In fact, advertising is already in the throes of discovering whether it can establish a "global brand."

The use of power of a third kind to develop global brands in the political realm is certain to be even more challenging and is just as certain to be tried. The very real potential for success does not just come from having global communications technology in the hands of only a few Western nations. One must add a high level of expertise to this technological advantage. In the West, this expertise has already formed into a remarkably sophisticated human communication system. An initial trial of that system already has begun. Indeed, those with their hands on this power are so certain of its viability they are already beginning to shift away from exclusive focus on older forms of coercion and force, persuasion and manipulation. They now pursue opportunities to use power of a third kind. An explication of the early outlines of this effort, along with an evaluation of its potential success and ramifications to non-Western countries, is the central narrative of this book.

It is not difficult to see power of a third kind as a discernible part of the current international discourse. In a non-insular world, international discourse is a powerful prism through which to view the ongoing contest for hegemony. With sophisticated planning and implementation, framing events ends in controlling how others interpret and explain them. Statement and restatement inevitably controls the questions and defines the allowable answers. Eventually, these frames become the structure of thought and discourse. Take human rights, for example. If a nation or group of nations successfully sells a definition of human rights that reflects their particular culture and political system, they have created a basis of rage in advance of their predictable need to stretch the envelope of acceptable actions. Then, when human rights' violations become a justification for isolating a nation, the basis of rage falls easily on those outside the definition they have created. This means that hegemony has moved from a nation's ability to *make* the rules to their ability to *validate* how well others adhere to the rules.

With power of a third kind in hand, it is hard to imagine any nation that would pass up the opportunity to make an evaluation of their actions fit their own interpretative frameworks. This book is about how that power has altered international discourse and how the unprecedented electronic media access offers opportunities to create a "new enemy" to justify the exceptionality Western nations have enjoyed over the past half-century.

A breakthrough in change demands a breakthrough in understanding the ramifications of that change. That breakthrough will come from non-Western nations only if they can understand, interpret, and screen the frameworks and narratives being put forward. This understanding must be based on an analysis able to illuminate the discovered trend of events to reveal the hidden pattern.

The world is in a delicate transition period. We do have institutions with the ability to interfere in the internal affairs of nations, for all the best reasons: hunger, internal strife, human rights abuses. However, the current approach to promoting democracy, protecting human rights and the environment are inadequate for two reasons. First, there is no clear global consensus on when, how, and by whom such intervention would take place. Second, control of those institutions that would be allowed to intervene by global consensus is in the hands of a few Western nations.

It is equally important that developing nations not be seen as uncritical supporters of democracy and human rights. As this book will show, Western powers are currently trying to establish themselves as the final "neutral" arbiters of all cases of intervention. These premises for intervention do not have global consensus. To uncritically support democracy and human rights, in the context of such self-serving Western premises, would be to subvert the process of debate and global consensus building. This can only lead to resentment and unproductive monologue.

True democracy, actual human rights accords, thoughtful protection of the environment, and care for the transgression of sovereignty can only take place within a context of true global dialogue. All nations must work for the recodification of human rights and freedoms and for minimum standards governing the appropriate conditions of international intervention. That dialogue of recodification must be derived from the rich diversity of all cultures, not just the exclusive cultural position of the most powerful nations.

As a biography of my own thought, this book reflects the transition it is analyzing and is, by necessity, a "thought in progress," a starting point for a renewed dialogue. It is an attempt to respond to the generic challenge of those intellectuals whose thought is not entirely constrained by their own or someone else's agenda. As such, it forces a pause and a distance between Western exertions of power to control the speed and complexity of change and non-Western attempts to deflect the impact these exertions have on indigenous cultural and political systems.

Chapter One of this book provides an insight into the major changes that most affect the alteration of human power in international relations. Particular attention is given to the impact of distance-destroying technology and to the emerging role of intellectuals in policy making, image shaping, and discourse control.

Chapter Two offers a layman's analysis of the emerging political economy of the media and how the systems around electronic communications will be used by the Western nations to project global political frames. Western intellectuals' experience in establishing the "free world" framework during the Cold War era is examined. This provides the context for analyzing how the Cold War inventory of ideological concepts will be used in a post-insular effort to create effective frameworks for exceptionality.

Chapter Three describes the character, the potential, and the challenge of any attempt to use power of a third kind. Had this book been written four or five years ago, there would not have been a good example of the attempt to use this power. Today, however, there is a laboratory of its use being patched together in the United States, an effort readily being followed in international discourse by other leading Western countries. These efforts offer a window into the way older policy and political elite systems are trying to shape a foreign policy around this newly emerging power. It allows a way of explicating how power of a third kind might be used by other nations.

Chapter Four outlines the criteria for a successful strategy and the way that the governmental and non-governmental institutional power of the West will be used to create these global frameworks. Because of their growing power and the clear trend of G8 countries away from majority-based international exposures, non-governmental organizations (NGOs) are intensively analyzed.

Chapter Five presents a preliminary analysis of the likely impacts on and alternative responses of developing nations to this use of power of a third kind. This analysis focuses on short- and long-term goals. In particular, this final chapter presents counterpower in this campaign as a source of strategy for non-Western nations that choose to actively participate. Finally, the counterpower of inaction is described and a program of active participation is developed.

NOTE

1. Herbert Rosinski, *Power and Human Destiny*, ed. Richard P. Stebbins (London: Pall Mall Press, 1965), 19. While I share Herbert Rosinski's opinion that power finds its source in the imaginative self, we differ on the definition of counterpower. Rosinski says that counterpower is the "bits of reality" that Man creates. I argue that counterpower is the reaction of others to exertions of power in the fluid intersubjectivity of Man's striving to impose his vision on the world.

POWER
OF A THIRD KIND

CHAPTER 1

Intentional Change Creates Power of a Third Kind

These thoughts are being written during a time of nearly incomprehensible change in human existence, human power, and global relations. Institutional relationships that, for centuries, have defined national identity suddenly appear questionable and strangely ambiguous. This is a "post" world—post-industrial and post-modern—where "de-institutionalization" has been elevated to acceptability and the demand for predictable order is derided as naïve and anachronistic. On the one hand, we are told not to hope for balance; rather, we are to become more comfortable with "dynamic imbalance." On the other hand, we are told that political change has ended. We are supposedly at the "end of history," and a single rationale for establishing a permanent world order has been found.

Not surprisingly, such a turbulent environment offers fertile ground for redefining all sorts of assumptions about our political world. The critical question is: Who will control the redefinition effort and what will be the terms of discussion? At base, we are talking about the unprecedented impact of distance-destroying technology on indigenous cultures. We also need to look at Western intellectuals, those arbitrators of discussion who will define how the advances in global communications will be used to shape and promote the policies of Western nations.

Our first inkling that change is not following the familiar patterns of global discourse were seen in the post–Cold War alterations in charters, conventions, and alliances within our political world. This aggressive international scrutiny and the resulting institutional change has been hailed and vilified as the "new world order." The accelerating pace of this conceptual transition threatens to outstrip the direction and character of change.

Human power, the primary source of change, has never been more promising and, paradoxically, never more in danger of being narrowed. Nature, once thought so frightening and mysterious, has become "knowable" as human intellect unlocks its structure and maps its terrain. Man's unique human capacity for imagination, creativity, and reflectivity has carried him to the point where Nature has become a set of facts to discover, sort, and store for easy access and retrieval. We are now in a transition where human nature has become the object of the same talents that made Nature so entirely knowable. The simulation of consciousness in technology has made this knowing and the capacity to manipulate human consciousness more readily available. Ironically, Man's ability to expand his innate talents at the moment he is realizing new abilities is narrowing these same talents.

During this transition, major changes occurring in all levels of human relations will necessarily command more attention. Disturbed by growing ramifications and impacts, concerned non-Western intellectuals are looking at the expanding communications and transportation systems with a sharpened eye. They have only recently recognized the importance of the fact that these technologies are being controlled by a very few people in a very small portion of the world. The dynamics of this centralization of distance-destroying technology represents the powerful underlying nature and character of change in the last half of the twentieth century. While human beings are quick to use the benefits of these miraculous technologies, they are slow to comprehend the impact such conveniences have on their lives and on their cultures.

From the standpoint of maintaining the indigenous diversity of cultures and the political choices they offer, this newly shaped arena of change differs from any that have preceded it. We are accustomed to change reflected in conflict over specific issues and individual policies. We must now prepare ourselves for conflict based on intellectual constructions of human beings, their nature, their process, and their power.

All nations have already had some experience with these constructions. In the nineteenth century, without the advantage of modern electronic communications, Marx and Engles tried to persuade world intellectuals and policy makers of historic determinism. Their presumption involved a single idea of Man, an unalterable pattern within which he would evolve, and a single method for knowing him, his nature, and his future. They argued that there is a pattern in class behavior and economic systems. They also argued that once a new world order is established through public control of the means of production, a predetermined course would be set leading inevitably to a political and economic utopia. This call for the world proletariat to revolt met with mixed success, both intellectually and politically. While communist leadership stifled protests of system injustice and struggled to gain the acquiescence of the masses, they offered expectations of a better life to be realized over time. But, the whole deterministic system—its ideology and its structure—collapsed when it failed to deliver.

With the advantages of electronic communications in the hands of a few Western nations, we are entering an age when Man's conquest of Nature has given him the confidence to invade the domain of Man himself. We now face this new world order, with "democracy" and "market democracy" standing victorious. This is an arena of knowledge with immeasurable complexity, where generalizations may lead to far-fetched conclusions and where misjudgments risk widespread and very dire consequences. The brief history of this invasion in the West leaves one with an uncomfortable sense that these efforts already have been partially successful in defining all humankind into a single method of knowing and into a single, inevitable pattern of change.

There is a need to alert developing world intellectuals to the fact that the effort to maintain cultural integrity has entered a new, more sophisticated phase. Intellectuals must stand back and take a long look at how they intend to protect their social and political institutions. Effective response to efforts to universalize Western political assumptions will require a more aggressive *non*-Western, rather than an *anti*-Western, response. Culturally loaded political concepts must be confronted on their own terms through the inherent strength of the same institutions that absorbed, and then discarded, other forms of Western ethnocentrism. In fact, non-Western cultures already are evolving political systems that promise to embrace a rapidly changing, ever more human world. But the pace of change in this transition is demanding a conceptual consensus and effective counter-strategies. This consensus and any new strategies must be able to cope with the speed, sophistication, and nuance of change catalyzed by a transparent effort to globalize Western political process.

There are instances in history when nations with fewer of the traditional assets of power have been able to resist foreign assessments and notions. In 1962, Algeria proved that it was neither French nor a part of France when it won independence. In 1956, Egypt proved that it could manage navigation in the Suez Canal without Western technicians and build the Aswan Dam without Western financial assistance. A virtual chorus of Western countries had predicted that the Egyptians would fail because such an undertaking just could not be done successfully by a developing country.

Saudi Arabia, too, proved wrong all those who contended that it could neither build industrial cities nor manage a petrochemical industry in a world full of experienced players in the petrochemical marketplace. In the two decades since that critical decision, Saudi Arabia has come to control seven percent of the world's petrochemical market and manage the world's largest oil exporting industry. In 1993, black and white South Africans proved that the oppressed and their former oppressors could govern together in peaceful cooperation. The economic success of other old Western colonies, such as Singapore and Malaysia and leading Asian nations like South Korea and Taiwan, are legendary even when periodic aberrations are taken into account.

Just as these developing nations once rejected the Western assumption of their inevitable failure, they must now reject intellectualized predictions of the ultimate demise of their cultural values and way of living. Doing this requires that developing nations have a common awareness as to the source, motivation, and nature of the Western platform for impacting non-Western cultures. They also must recognize that there is the very real potential for developing nations to grasp their own future. Taking control of the future can best be achieved by focusing on what non-Western nations are able to offer rather than on what they can counter. Control cannot be achieved without a clear consensus within each nation's culture about those conditions most supportive to maintaining the diverse spiritual and moral systems within and between nations.

Successfully accomplishing this common awareness demands that the developing world understand contemporary human power as it is. Such understanding begins with a working knowledge of the generic and contemporary relationship between and among human beings in this non-insular world. By controlling global communications and international institutions, certain Western nations can now penetrate all cultures and nations. If successful in this effort, the relationship between nations will be entirely Western in construction.

An early manifestation in the use of this concentration of power is the "market democracy" campaign initiated by the United States and followed by other major Western nations. As a global political campaign, it is totally without historic precedent and is thoroughly ethnocentric. For non-Western nations, facing this challenge requires a critical analysis of the power of carefully constructed symbols. This power cannot be comprehended by associating it with old-time "propaganda" or the symbolic puffery typical of the Cold War ideological contest. For non-Western countries desiring democracy as their political system of choice, this campaign may in fact threaten the substantive accomplishment of their goal. Since Western nations do not have democracy as a true objective in the first place, the symbolic use of "democracy" and "free markets" as vehicles for achieving preeminence threatens the realization of both.

Currently, the "North-South" or "East-West" dialogue is neither critical nor a true dialogue. It is a monologue, a one-way communication from West to East, North to South, with more power and real impact than any mobilized bias[1] in history. Neither is there a truly critical dialogue between and among non-Western nations. Because the non-Western nations do not enjoy a sophistication, projection, or access to power equal to the West, demonizing Western cultures is just another monologue notable for its irrelevance to participation in global discourse.

Non-Western nations must be aware of a simple, overarching historical fact: They have lost the comfortable protection of insularity and, with it, any hope of confronting change by censorship or closed discourse. If non-Western nations do not respond effectively to the minute-by-minute projection of Western assumptions about human beings, human behavior, human power, and human political process, the general undermining of the diversity of all non-Western cultures will be the inevitable result.

DISTANCE NO LONGER PROTECTS CULTURE

Like other eras before us, we share the compelling human need to create new technological responses to the human environment and then to respond to the impact of that technology. Advances in weapons technology defined the twentieth century with nuclear arms capable of destroying all life on the planet. However, having barely comprehended the concept of the nuclear endgame, Man enters the twenty-first century confronting the "information explosion." In the last five decades, advanced transportation and communications technology have destroyed distance and, with it, any hope for maintaining cultural insularity in a world already comfortable with switching channels and getting "on-line."

As a young man, the amazing reality was being able to board a plane and quickly travel to any point on the globe. Now, to travel the world in "real" time, we do not even need to leave our favorite chair. Our small planet is accessible to anyone capable of pressing a channel changer or computer key with his index finger. This all but total unlocking of Nature's secrets ends in leaving Man's cultures and nations without many secrets. The latest penetration of Nature's frontiers has opened wide once exotic boundaries in human cultural diversity. In less than three decades, it has become possible for a single individual to visually experience almost the entire topography of human existence.

Until very recently, experiencing "the world" as anything more than an abstract concept was impossible. Making decisions with "the world" as a point of departure was stated as a rhetorical gesture, but for most people "the world" was limited to their own country or, at most, their own region. Today, it is virtually impossible to live in the world and not take the entire world into account. In matters from marketing and finance to political and social decisions, individual and institutional responses require a global focus. The reality of very real communities of people from around the world functioning within sight and sound of one another forces us to take a more global view.

We must not be circumspect on this point. When, for the first time, each and every culture is forced to take other cultures into account, even the most conservative commentator should not hesitate in calling this a watershed era in the lives of human beings. The destruction of physical distance does not, on its own, presage the destruction of cultural difference. However, it does signal the potential for creating a platform for change in the consciousness of people once safely insulated within the assumptions of their indigenous cultures.

It is no longer possible for any one person, group, or nation to be utterly insular when an entire world of difference cannot help but be known. This fact requires a different perspective on such terms as "culture" and "ethnocentrism." These terms were developed when insularity was the norm. In such a period, there were often cultural conflicts with one ethnocentrism pitted against the other—both within nations and across borders. Differences in culture were seen as serious but transitory problems of concern in the planning of a nation's economic, political, or military strategy. But today, in a world shrunk to the size of a neighborhood, exotic perceptions of Man, the planet, and international relations are no longer appropriate. Man is already moving beyond global reach, out of the "global village," and into the once unimaginable experience of "global consciousness." Global communications, while not yet reaching every individual in every part of this global village, already impacts every world leader and much of the world elite. In essence, when we are talking about ways of defending, maintaining, and expanding indigenous cultures, the destruction of distance is the difference that makes all the difference. It is also the single most important catalyst for deciding the global vision children today will be living under tomorrow.

When faced with the capacity of powerful nations to transcend indigenous systems, the real concern is with a more politically charged scenario. This scenario alters physical human conditions into mercurial terms loaded with the ethnocentric values of a certain "concerned" culture. Given the convergence of historic circumstances and technology, it would be naïve not to recognize that democracy, human rights, a clean environment, and other such laudable constructs are usable as vehicles to achieve Western political and economic ends. The call for critical dialogue within intellectual circles of the developing world is not an attack on those that yearn for or, indeed, work for the betterment of the human condition. Nearly any effort that expands the power of human beings' striving should be supported. However, we cannot afford to be naïve about the potential political impact of such rhetorical manipulation on receiving nations. At a minimum, that support must be based on the need to protect the integrity of culturally derived processes and institutions against attempts to create a single political agenda.

One need not spend much time asking whether the aggressive imposition of such an agenda and its symbolic rationalization is "good" or "bad." It simply is. By the very nature of his striving, Man will always take advantage of every opportunity to impose a self-serving vision on the world and will strive to make it an institutionalized reality. This is not a cynical view of power. It simply recognizes the way striving human beings interact in the human world. All leaders must be concerned with "good" and "bad," "moral" and "immoral." However, "labeling" rarely leads to real power. Non-Western nations will only find power by treating such aggressive efforts as matters of political and social choice. These choices require effective responses that can only be made in terms of the needs, knowledge, and resources of their own countries. Standing in one's own culture shaking one's head at the queer and "wrong" behavior of another culture may offer temporary relief in a confusing world. But it will do little or nothing to maintain the strength of one's own culture in the face of such power.

These are different times. They demand different perceptions. Global perceptual reach necessarily creates unprecedented arenas of co-operation and conflict. On a macro level, human beings are re-defining the source of their power, their uniquely human self, and the proper lines of transaction between individuals and their institutions. Hoping for objectivity and neutrality in the struggle of Man to define human knowing and human power is useless because those controlling the definitions have far too much to gain.

This is a contest for nothing less than control of the interpretative and imaginative powers of the human mind in areas of political process and cultural alternative. Success in establishing a universal Western culture can only be achieved by restricting cultural diversity and political choice among non-Western nations. Such restrictions would limit them to Western constructs and to copying Western institutions. If the West can accomplish this, the prize they win will be the ability to define "appropriate" and "acceptable" actions among world nations to fit Western political and economic agendas.

CULTURE IS MORE THAN "ACTS AND ARTIFACTS"

To adequately face the challenges of Western efforts to universalize its culture, our perception of culture must be adjusted to fit the new "global reach." With more and more of the world literally blanketed with the artifacts of human productivity, culture must be seen for what it is: the central arena of political striving and, simultaneously, the main instrument of interaction and reaction, of integration and discord. Culture has come popularly to connote those objects and ways of living that differentiate one group from another. Such an "object-focused" interpretation of culture was more appropriate to an insular world. A contemporary understanding of the new arena of human strife requires the realization that culture is not simply manifested in act and artifact. Culture today is the collective and dynamically active perspectives of living individuals,[2] perspectives that will be shaped by the symbolic use of terms like "market democracy" and "human rights."

This change in our perception of culture is at the heart of any use of power of a third kind in today's non-insular world. While the non-Western nations' culture of monologue devolves into irrelevance, developed nations' institutional relationships are all expanding in response to advances in transportation and communication. Because this technology was created and developed in terms of the resources and values of its creators, developed nations were the first to realize its positive advantages and could most readily adapt to the new vehicle in more powerful ways. Particularly important is that the grammar of the media is increasingly reflected in the timing and the discourse of the political institutions on which it is supposedly only reporting. The power of communications technology catalyzes a mirroring effect, the result of which has a "centralizing" impact on the policy and strategic decisions of the commercial, government, and media entities using the technology. As in all human striving, the power of intent shapes itself to the power of its most effective vehicle.

At conferences or international meetings, developing nation intellectuals do not always see such newly emerging susceptibility as a serious threat. To them it seems like an old story they have heard before, a story that has proven itself largely untrue. They remember dire predictions about the loss of their cultures certain to come from modernization. These predictions were found to be projections of the Western experience, an experience the West assumed was a necessary part of all development. Despite such ominous foreboding, newly developing countries with the will and the wherewithal continued on with their chosen destinies. They went ahead and modernized their societies, created a better standard of living, and replaced consultant technicians with nationals. Change of all kinds did, of course, occur. However, a substantive erasure of traditional ways of viewing the world simply did not happen.

The danger of such lessons from the past is that they simply have little to do with the last thirty years, much less with the next half century. Given the current undoing of insularity, such anachronistic thinking and the resulting complacency is the most powerful enemy working against the protection and expansion of the rich diversity of non-Western cultures. If one cannot see the difference in the global situation between 1979 and 1999, there is no chance that the dramatic import of the current Western threat will be grasped in time to confront the incremental undermining of cultures.

Again, we must look beyond the important but transitory conflict over individual issues that create crises across the globe on a nearly daily basis. We must look toward practical impacts resulting from the communication of a certain concept of Man and, in particular, a certain concept of human political choice. Finally, and most importantly, it must be admitted that such an effort could well be successful despite all the obvious fissures in the consensus and stability of the West. The living nature of cultural perceptions is such that, even if the West were to abandon its campaign, the worldwide communications power would continue to communicate the very assumptions the West has abandoned. The constructed systems could totally fail in actual practice but still be very successful as frameworks supporting Western political exceptionality.

THE MOTIVATION BEHIND THE GLOBAL CAMPAIGN

Many non-Western nations, faced with the complexity and enormity of this campaign, ask a simple question: What drives all this effort? The answer to this question is vitally important. In the West, there is a growing sense that something deep in the structure of things has simply let go. There is a sense of an empty space, a hiatus where the pattern of meaning presented by Western intellectuals to comprehend the events of the world has been stretched beyond its capacities. It is as though the would-be Western planner of the project returned to his work and mistakenly skipped several pages. The planner goes on but those being planned for hold back, suddenly confronted with a chasm between expectations and reality. For these people, the framework of dependable meaning appears to be shredding too much in the present to maintain confidence that it will be durable very far into the future.

Imagining—let alone understanding—the oncoming massiveness of the drive to universalize Western culture is not really possible without understanding the true depths of concern being felt among its leaders. To comprehend this, one must grasp the shock of Western elites when the availability of resources did not match the assumption of Western exceptionality. With uncommon suddenness, this collection of culturally similar nations was faced with an entirely ahistorical inability to find vital resources or to control critical markets.

Nothing less than the nearly sacred assumption of a middle-class way of life for everyone willing to work for it was and still is being questioned. This questioning created doubt about the larger assumption of Western exceptionality. When a middle-class way of life for everyone else in the world was not predictable, it was peripherally disturbing. When attaining an exceptional standard of living became problematic for the West, it was a powerful force able to call the entire belief in Western exceptionality into review.

For several centuries, Western nations have sincerely believed that the largess they had wrung from Nature was made possible by their idealized beliefs. Only in the last few decades of this century have these sociopolitical assumptions been tested. They were thrown into doubt when the traditional Western sources of power failed to provide the support necessary to maintain the world's highest levels of consumption.

Immediately following World War II, the Western belief system and the real world of commerce, resources, and growth all seemed to affirm one another. It is not entirely cynical to say that, for a time, saving the world while promoting Western evolutionary history as the prototype of all modern human history was a very profitable business. Too soon, however, "doing well by doing good" began to suffer reversals. Nearly by the month, it became strikingly more costly and less politically beneficial to maintain the belief system. One after another, the export of "free trade," "human rights," "democracy," and more recently, "save the planet" treaties were found to be both counterproductive, in terms of cost, and an embarrassment when the media spotlight revealed the disturbing state of all these qualities in the very nations promoting them.

To make matters worse, geophysical Nature itself began to appear woefully unaware of a progress scenario that placed developed countries at the center of production and consumption. Resources and markets were often as badly placed as they were desperately needed. In particular areas and, to varying degrees, distance-destroying technology could come to the rescue. Often this technology was so efficient that supplies could be transported and manufactured more cheaply by others than they could be purchased domestically. This partial solution continues in operation, with varying success, until this moment. Meanwhile, domestic political and social tension increases while less and less access to non-domestic resources can be gained by traditional means or with traditional assumptions of exceptionality.

Consider the situation: Being the largest industrial and military power brought with it significant control of international political and financial institutions. As resource-holding nations became more sophisticated at playing the game inside and outside of institutions, such easy access to resources could not always be leveraged through traditional means. Without these leverages, the only power left was that of international agenda-setting primed around Western values and supported by already existing military and institutional resources. But even this was not entirely adequate. Due to the increasing sophistication of nations able to see through the script of the bi-polar narrative, a more compelling story was required. The mismatch of rhetoric and substance in Western nations' foreign policy was already undermining the effectiveness of exceptionality as a means of maintaining access to resources and strategic alliances.

Simply stated, the older exchanges for exceptional treatment involved capital and resources as well as promised protection from the "evil empire." In the post–Cold War, post-insular period, this exchange was, in the first instance, no longer affordable and, in the second, no longer credible. Within a faltering rationale for exceptionality, failing markets and access to resources were made more problematic by a sudden scarcity in the amount of time available for revamping domestic economic strategy. The key catalyst was the stunning resurgence of Asia as an economic power.

There was and is no time for celebrating the end of the Cold War. Western nations simply cannot start over. They have to work with the remains of a forty-year investment in Cold War technology and ideology. To limit both risk and cost, Western nations must refocus on the nature of the exchange, taking into account the powerful Western system for the production and dissemination of knowledge. This system has three key elements: First, the proliferation of Western objects throughout the globe is nearly total. Second, knowledge, product creation, and dissemination are already a rationalized and highly interactive social, political, and economic system directly connected to the market economy. Third, these two systematized contextual realities are transformed into political power by an emerging group of political professionals and bureaucratized intellectuals. This highly charged context is the everyday workshop of Western intellectuals across the full spectrum of policy making, business, and media. They enjoy a half-century's experience of wielding sophisticated analysis, discourse creation, and motivational techniques in the promotion of values and constructs—all in a process where selling soup and selling ideology hardly differ in technique or implementation.

INTELLECTUALS: GIVING THE TEXT
TO CONTEXT

In this global campaign, a framework for thought is being constructed. Such a framework encompasses the issues discussed previously and gives them shape and definition. Understanding the current and future political terms used to justify Western exceptionality—"progress," "modernization," "democracy," "human rights," and so forth—is not possible without understanding that they are constructs created by Western intellectuals. These terms were created out of a set of premises, in terms of a certain logic, and rendered into quite compelling narratives. This logic and the resulting strategy will be entirely missed and misunderstood if one thinks about this consciousness-changing effort in terms of single, easily recognized issues.

There probably is no better example of how these intellectually constructed concepts can drive a pervasive set of Western assumptions than is found in the term "progress." Mid-nineteenth-century "system builders" were intent on making the term "more readily satisfy the contemporary criteria of a science."[3] Once enshrined in the intellectual's list of first principles, such a truism becomes a vehicle for the justification of exceptionality for whatever entity is powerful enough to use it. This point of power occurs when such a symbolic concoction becomes a part of the commonsense discourse of everyday life. Once that happens, its power belongs to those that can capture it and make it identified with their own identities and strategies.

From these intellectual machinations around the concept of "progress," all cultures were made greater or lesser victims of an avalanche of ethnocentric discourse. Growth by stages was at the vanguard of a supposedly natural and linear pattern inevitable for all men. This narrative, along with its cultural values and political and economic systems, presented Western science as universal. Once decorated with the badge of scientific neutrality, the stages of growth theory was granted universality not only as a description of progress, but effectively as a description of Man himself. Progress, rather than describing what Man did, became what Man *must do*, and then what Man *ought to do*. Stages of growth was no longer *outside* of Man's individual actions. It was now placed *inside* Man as an *inherent* part of his nature.

In this way, human progress was elevated from a description of intentionally created change to an unquestioned process inherent to all human beings. Progress, as represented in Western societies and identified with their history and culture, became the measuring stick for all cultures. When the measuring stick was applied, the distinction between "traditional" societies and "modern" societies was derived. Now, it was only by moving along the the stages of growth path that societies could progress into modernity. This theory of modernization has lost favor, but new constructions are currently being brought forward in contemporary Western political discourse. As we shall see, the new constructions are not essentially different from the old: They are still sited *within* Man, placing political process outside Man's choice and outside of indigenous political process.

Awed by military technology and distracted by the clamor of episodic crises, non-Western nations often get a distorted view of the highly intellectualized origins and systematized technique of Western foreign policy. There are four aspects of intellectual enterprise in the Western foreign policy system that must be comprehended: first, the nature of intellectual work in Western nations and the historic bureaucratization of the intellectual; second, the fluid changeability and rhetorical power of intellectualized knowledge; third, the division of labor and the roles of each of the varieties of bureaucratized intellectual; and fourth, the role of intellectuals in the forming of foreign policy.

Historically, the intellectual's social and political role has been, on the surface, relatively well understood. The intellectual is involved in "the interpretation of and commentary on the experiences of contemporary life, including the dissemination of such commentary to an audience or audiences. . . . His tools are words and other symbols . . . while his technologies are the machinery, organizations, and processes designed to accumulate and to publicize"[4] the results of his work. But the essential differentiating fact is his "mediating role between the reality that he experiences and the constructions of that reality that guide thought and conduct in society at large."[5]

The key terms here are "mediator," "constructions," and "guide." Rarely in a decision-making role, the modern intellectual is, nevertheless, in an interdependent role with decision makers. Through his extensive access to and understanding of knowledge and knowledge process, he mediates in his bureaucratized role between what is known and a leader's need to create, communicate, and implement policy. In his role as mediator, the intellectual actively organizes knowledge in such a way that the resulting construction guides and shapes the policy, its use, and its acceptability.

In government foreign policy, this description of the intellectual as mediator has, in the West, also evolved into the role of advocate. The Western intellectual advocates policy and he advocates positions, economically and politically, in the interests of his expanding professional group. He is part of a group of individuals who have an elite status—in fact, often more status than real power. There is a discernible sociology here. Inside this sociology, there is an assumption that the thoughts, discoveries, or understandings they come upon will be of value to society and should be communicated to it. Ironically, however, because the intellectuals underestimate the intelligence of the masses and the masses assume that the product of the intellectuals' labor has little relevance to their everyday lives, there is not a routine meeting place for discourse. In the end, these Western intellectuals, once thought to be defenders of citizens against the force of government, rarely communicate with ordinary people. In fact, personally and professionally, they communicate almost entirely with elites.

The journey toward scientism taken by Western intellectuals began during the Enlightenment when knowledge, itself, was "captured" by scientific method, which in turn became the basis for Western institutions' success and continuing status. Being exclusionary in its initial assumptions, it left little or no ground for speculative or spiritual knowledge. It was a matter of join in or be left out. The decision to join has trapped the Western intellectual for over three centuries. To understand policy making and the role of intellectuals in that process, it is important to have an idea of how this entrapment came about. Inherent in that historical experience is an understanding of the way Cold War policy has developed and the way the future campaign for Western exceptionality will evolve.

Over three centuries ago, intellectuals created knowledge about knowing, identified that knowledge with the physicality of Nature, and then applied its premises and criteria to all previously accepted ways of knowing about human experience. From that time until today, scientism, as a philosophy and a way of thinking, continues to be transcendent. While Western intellectuals often pursue intensely spiritual lives, only "scientifically" derived conclusions are readily given credibility in most matters of social, political, and economic import. This attitude is held to the extent that reason is seen as not "anything more than the ability to think scientifically." This affirms then that the "norms and benefits" of technology as the child of science "can be transported into social life with equally 'rational' results."[6]

The achievement of such perceptual centrality was hardly a purely scholarly or an objective act. Rather, it was a political act with all the vagaries of any common grab for comparative leverage. From the latter part of the Medieval period, this aggressive movement took on the character of an attack on institutions whose foundations were already sociologically and politically shaky. These entities were prime targets for political aggression as a result of the rigidity of their assumptions and the inflexibility of their social hierarchy.

Scientific method, the main totem of scientism, ruled out acceptance of knowledge products that had not been limited to sense data and barred such activity as speculative and imaginative ruminations. These latter modes of creation were derided as idle curiosity and labeled as being "non-sense." Once institutionalized, scientifically acceptable knowing was ritualized into demands that all conclusions be "replicable" and "quantifiable." In this way, both the interpretative and imaginative powers of human individuals were conscripted into the scientistic effort. The production resulting from ways of knowing that did not follow these institutionalized precepts went either unrecognized or were simply discounted and placed on the periphery of "true" knowledge. In effect, the spiritual and even the artistic side of Man's gestures toward other men or the world were set aside by a critique that seemed bent on narrowing the power of human consciousness. Knowledge producers who did not follow the screening criteria were made lovingly eccentric and, ultimately, irrelevant.

Such an attack on the interpretive human self was bound to entrap all those who acquiesced to its full logic. In the end, intellectuals were, themselves, confounded by the very knowledge production process they promoted. It is quite easy to see how the Western intellectual fell into this waiting trap. What one writer calls the "bigamous marriage"[7] between science and the intellectual ended in undermining the intellectual as a creative force in society. He was consumed by scientific method bureaucratized within its sundry institutions, from industry to government to foundations. Once a single way of knowing was sanctified as the *only* way of knowing, it alone became deserving of substantial resources.

The intellectual found that credibility was only possible if he could prove that the knowledge he produced had been arrived at in the same manner scientifically sanctioned by technical people. The Western intellectual found that he needed the cloak of neutral objectivity. The more he sought to affect such an image, the more he was absorbed by institutionalized science. In this way, willingly, but often unwittingly, he joined an institution committed by its very nature to narrowing all thinking to utilitarianism, scientism, and "first principles."

Science was pressing upon one and all the need to work toward final principles that would predict the behavior of whatever was being studied. Because social, political, and psychological scholars were dealing with people, they were more hard pressed than those dealing with redundant and logical Nature. Instead of arguing that such a precept did not fit with a creature who was imaginative, creative, and self-reflective with the unnerving quality of volition, social thinkers and scholars decided to become "social scientists." After all, their roles as mediators would be lost if their knowledge was not given the same status as the people who were producing the turbine engine and the electric toaster.

This decision was, in many cases, one of conviction; however, given their situation, it was never devoid of political and economic necessity. Largely as a result of the success of science itself, they were already placed outside the gates by the ecclesiastical order; they had always been shunned or marginalized as irrelevant by the middle class. If not for the sufferance of government and industry elite, they would have disappeared as a necessary occupation. Turning themselves into scientists promised to return them to a familiar role. This time though, due to the arbitrary rules of science, there was the promise of a much more powerful role than that of mediator. Once the social sciences were accepted as "sciences," intellectuals could become the judges of which institutions were promoting the natural "objective" state of Man and which were blocking Man from the realization of his natural evolutionary pattern. Once again, the magic would be in the intellectuals' hands but now, to the status of eccentric thinker, they would add the more powerful roles of judges and protectors.

The intellectual offspring of this marriage between the intellectual and science are, today, everywhere in Europe and America and, unfortunately, in the general images of the future held by the developing world. Consider intellectuals in the American news media: "Objectivity also became a selling point as public discourse in the United States shifted from a Christian to a scientific paradigm of legitimation."[8] As one critic observed: "Although journalists may not be aware of it, they are perhaps the strongest remaining bastion of logical positivism in America."[9] Thus intellectuals of all types are bureaucratized into a specialized social and political system capable of producing and disseminating narrow knowledge products with heretofore unimagined speed, efficiency, and mindnumbing serialism.

Once joined with the growing ranks of the physical and biological scientists, Western intellectuals became the cutting edge for an all-out attack on the self as a source of human power. Simple or complex speculation about other men, or indeed, thoughts a Man might have about his own self and his world condition were denigrated as "mentalistic" or opinionated—most of all not scientific. The net result of all of this screening, cutting, and slashing of Man's imaginative potential was an abrupt narrowing of the kinds of questions that could be legitimately asked and the types of conclusions that could be credibly offered. Once the initiator of entirely new concepts, Western intellectuals had ceased asking mankind to even consider new orders of facts as salient and relevant to the concerns of knowledge altogether. Nor did they ask for a vision of Man that could carry him forward during an increasingly more complex period. Why? In a process revealed only to a small group of political or social scientists possessed of a single way of knowing what is "true," Western Man is assumed to be "already there."

Bureaucratized, intellectuals no longer presented their interpretations and constructs to the world as idiosyncratic interpretations of an individual or social group. Instead, the work of intellectuals was increasingly determined by the institutions that controlled both their status and their funding.[10] Where once intellectuals used their access to leaders to reach the masses, now government, business, and media leaders use the intellectuals' critical and communicative abilities to reach the masses.

In the end, Western intellectuals became a part of a very tightly woven system. Like all systems, it has a certain internal logic. This systemic structure persistently draws more and more power and involvement into itself. The intrinsic rhythm of funding and strict criteria for acceptable methodology results in a bureaucratized effort toward gaining the "truth." The need for scientific verification and the affirmation of those following scientific criteria draws the intellectual ever deeper into the economic and political imperatives of the governmental, institutional, and corporate center. Because they were no longer political advisers but political "scientists," the intellectuals could do anything physicists could do except apply for a patent. Confident in and comfortable with scientism, governments have not hesitated to spend an increasing amount of money on these social theorists turned "scientists." In the United States, federal spending for social science research in

1951 was $6 million; in 1971 it was $421 million; and estimates for the early 1980s varied from $1 billion to $2 billion per annum, not including state and local governments.[11] This rate of spending continues to escalate.

This dramatic absorption of the intellectual has not gone without notice. The best of Western social analysts exhibit a grinding doubt about their scientific approach to social knowledge and the value of the knowledge products they currently churn out. Nevertheless, the unquestioned investment of these social theorists and critics in such concepts as modernization and development generally finds little disconfirmation. At the same time, bureaucratic rewards are dispensed to those social scientists whose subjects and conclusions fall within such constructs.

When non-Western countries assess Western foreign policy strategy, they make three perceptual mistakes about the role of Western intellectuals in the formation of that policy. First, some assume the experience of their own policy making, with its minimal dependence on intellectuals as mediators, concept creators, or symbol manipulators, when gauging the intensity of Western foreign policy analysis. Second, non-Western nations often fail to recognize that the sociology of intellectuals operating in and out of government think tanks, social networks, and knowledge production systems is highly sophisticated, competitive, and interactive. Third, they cannot imagine why any government would want to spend so much money on symbol manipulation.

As long as the knowledge production component of intellectual influence remains misunderstood and underestimated, non-Western nations' decision making will not find itself up to the current and future levels of transnational cultural activism. Nor could they comprehend power of a third kind. There is no need for conspiracy theory here. The West simply enjoys a mature propaganda system developed over the half-century since World War II. It is a significant resource that has proven its efficacy and will be used as the only viable response to domestic and global circumstances. Developing nations must understand that when such incorporated and bureaucratized intellectuals arrive in a developing country, scientific objectivity and issue representation are only an outward posture. These intellectuals represent their own agenda.

For example, the entire assortment of institutionalized Western assumptions may be found in the seemingly benevolent concern shown by intellectuals for the welfare of peoples of the developing world. This "concern" has a syntax and a rationale that is thoroughly consistent with a Western concept of Man and society. Western non-governmental organizations (NGOs) work diligently to get into the now trendy grass roots of a country and insist that they are approaching an indigenous society with multicultural objectivity. However, one need only scratch the surface to find an overriding consensus around what all men *should be* and the role individuals and nations *should take* to attain a more "natural" and "progressive" human society.

Underneath it all is the transparent and particularistic historical experience of Western culture; namely, that "the individual, not an institution, is the source of moral judgment; experience, not tradition, is the source of understanding. . . . 'Authentic identity' is the norm . . . institutional and organizational life . . . is inherently depersonalizing and destructive of the 'whole man.' "[12] Western transnational discourse is actually a blend of several themes: Western missionary altruism; disregard for the philosophical and moral assumptions of most non-Western societies; and a mostly presumptuous perception that, even if mistakes are made, people of developing nations will still be better off than in their "backward" state.

When developing societies are seen as having difficulties, such problems are cited as examples of the inherent instability of nations fighting the supposed backwardness of traditional institutions. Purportedly, such non-progressive societies are so hooked on outdated tradition, they are unable to meet the challenge of change. Always implied, of course, is the phrase "like we have done." Such visitors rarely question their own equations and their own political and social assumptions. When the West has problems from inflation to riots, such difficulties are seen as a "managerial dysfunction" quite susceptible to the tinkering of home-based technicists. The veracity of Western political culture is assumed as the standard. The only real problem is the capacity of people to take full advantage of the system or to pursue the dictates of that system within the Western vision of justice and common sense.

INTELLECTUALS AS CREATORS OF POLICY

In the United States, the bureaucratization of the intellectual began in the Great Depression when so many were needed to fill all the agencies of the government. Their numbers increased after World War II in response to the demands of the Marshall Plan and the Truman Doctrine.[13] Finding people to fill this need was not a problem. Academic institutions of all kinds were bursting at the seams with brilliant, well-schooled historians, political scientists, and economists eager to test their theories on the world scene, ready to be a part of the history they were quite tired of teaching.

After that they just stayed on, filling government agencies—especially the State Department—with bureaucratized intellectuals. If they were not working at the State Department, the Pentagon, or the CIA, they could ply their trade among the many corporate, institutional, or media entities. Many did not even have to leave academia to participate in the making of history. "A survey of top academics (those 2,500 American professors who are members of major academies or honorific societies)[found] that one-fourth had advised either the president or cabinet and sub-cabinet officers or both, and over two-thirds had served as consultants to government agencies."[14] The best and the brightest had no problem adjusting because, particularly in foreign policy, the upper levels of executive bureaucracy lacked a global world view. Incrementally, domestic politicians became dependent upon the intellectuals' foreign policy knowledge.

American intellectuals' involvement in foreign and military policy-related concepts and ideas does not stand in academic isolation from policy. Indeed, "this body of ideas had significant effects on the policy of the United States government."[15] In essence, "they have helped create the conceptual framework and the framework of ideas in which both domestic and foreign/military policy were constructed."[16] This flow from longer-term conceptualization begins with members of the society of intellectuals, including government, corporate, media, and institutions. From and through them the flow proceeds in dynamically interactive feedback loops. In this way, constructs like "containment," "domino theory," "end of history," and "clash of civilizations" begin to gain acceptance within the decision-making apparatus and gain exposure in the media. Initially, they are a part of the treatment used in actual situations. Then they become a basis of bureaucratized judgmental criteria regarding the participation and performance of people and other entities in wider numbers of situations.

The sociology of foreign-policy making has a politics and an elite structure. In foreign-policy creation, there are essentially three groups of active intellectuals: the "clerisy," protectors of what is; the "policy intellectuals," experts relied upon by elites or government to form policy and action; and "the ideological intellectuals," who are the activators of ideas and values, and the defenders of institutions.[17] These three levels are never completely distinct to the extent that communication is foreclosed by status boundaries alone. A high-frequency and high-fidelity communication network exists within a discernible society holding shared cultural assumptions and similar social, educational, and economic backgrounds. The surface of petty conflict hides a very interactive and highly involved elite where intellectuals on all levels—whether temporarily in or out of political power—meet with equanimity and within a remarkably tight consensus.

Since World War II, the propagation of Western values have been so much a part of the discourse and the context of developed nations' rhetoric that many leaders and intellectuals assume they are now immune to its effects. However, as this book attempts to demonstrate, when a few incomparably powerful nations have virtual control over electronic communications, de facto control of international institutions, and an inventory of equally incomparable military and ideological resources, there is, indeed, a "new story" with potentially quantum differences in impact on developing countries.

The Western programs tailored for the developing world—from aid to technical assistance—have always been framed in ethnocentric narratives. Today, however, this mobilization of ethnocentric symbols justifying Western involvement in non-Western countries is a primary, not a secondary part of Western strategy. To critical observers, the projection and the manipulation of a single view of history, political culture, and the future are now thoroughly transparent as the West strives to maintain its position of global hegemony. Ironically and ominously, non-Western nations find themselves in a period of history where a few powerful nations depend on their acquiescence to the assumption that they need Western protection, guidance, and, in effect, a Western way of life.

Non-Western leaders find it difficult to imagine a grand global strategy precisely because they have never participated in it; they have only been the targets of such a campaign. In this case, they must get up to date with the post-modern world and understand that soon most developed countries will begin to channel their resources into a focus on controlling the global discourse. If developing nations want to move from targets and spectators to actual participants, they must do more than just join "the Club." They must work to include their own version of the roles, rules, and rituals of international participation within a vision constructed by all nations.

It must not be assumed, however, that the whole contest of power of a third kind is solely between developed and developing nations. Right now, the United States is only the first Western nation to engage in power of a third kind; they are the only nation equal to the task. However, there are signs that France is not entirely willing to step aside while the United States attempts to gain exceptional access to markets through ideological projection, military intervention, and institutional manipulation.

As with all contests, needs, knowledge, and resources will create the underlying force of competition even among those sharing similar assumptions and values. Clearly, however, America will be the early test case for the use of power of a third kind. As such, its policy formation and implementation provides an early paradigm for non-Western nation analysts. Even in these days of transition to this more aggressive ideological effort, the strategy, the reasons for doing it, and the rationale that will guide that effort are apparent enough to begin to articulate a non-Western nation response.

NOTES

1. For a discussion of mobilized bias, see E. E. Schattschneider, *The Semisovereign People: A Realist's View of Democracy in America* (New York: Holt, Rinehart and Winston, 1960). Also, see John B. Thompson, "Mass Communication and Modern Culture: Contribution to a Critical Theory of Ideology," *Sociology* 22 (August 1988): 359–83.

2. For a thorough analysis of self and culture in line with this analysis, see Anthony P. Cohen, *Self-Consciousness: An Alternative Anthropology of Identity* (New York: Routledge, 1994).

3. Michael Foley, "Progress," in *Ideas that Shape Politics*, ed. Michael Foley (Manchester, England: Manchester University Press, 1994), 212.

4. Jay Weinstein, "The Third World and Developmentalism: Technology, Morality, and the Role of the Intellectual," in *The Mythmakers: Intellectuals and the Intelligentsia in Perspective*, ed. Raj P. Mohan, International Journal of Contemporary Sociology, Contributions in Sociology, Number 63 (New York: Greenwood Press, 1987), 111.

5. Ibid.

6. Peter Nettl, "Power and the Intellectuals," in *Power and Consciousness*, eds. Conor Cruise O'Brien and William Dean Vanech (London: University of London Press Ltd., 1969), 21.

7. J. P. Nettl, "Ideas, Intellectuals, and Structures of Dissent," in *On Intellectuals*, ed. Philip Rieff (Garden City, N.Y.: Doubleday and Co., 1969), 99.

8. Thomas Roach, "Competing News Narratives, Consensus, and World Power," in *The U.S. Media and the Middle East: Image and Perception*, ed. Yahya R. Kamalipour, Contributions to the Study of Mass Media and Communications Number 46 (Westport, Conn.: Greenwood Press, 1995), 27.

9. Ibid., quoting Herbert J. Gans, *Deciding What's News: A Study of CBS Evening News, NBC Nightly News, Newsweek and Time* (New York: Vintage Books, 1979), 184.

10. Weinstein, "The Third World and Developmentalism," 112.

11. Eva Etzioni-Halevy, *The Knowledge Elite and the Failure of Prophecy* (London: George Allen & Unwin, 1985), 22.

12. Daniel Bell, "The New Class: A Muddled Concept," in *The New Class?*, ed. B. Bruce-Briggs (New Brunswick, N.J.: Transaction Books, 1979), 186.

13. Theodore Draper, "Intellectuals in Politics," *Encounter* 49 (1977): 51, cited in Etzioni-Halevy, *The Knowledge Elite*, 19–20.

14. Etzioni-Halevy, *The Knowledge Elite*, 22, referring to Seymour M. Lipset, "The Academic Mind at the Top," *Public Opinion Quarterly* 46 (1982): 150.

15. R. E. Licklider, "Policy Scientists and Nuclear Weapons," in *The Use and Abuse of Social Science*, ed. I. L. Horowitz (New Brunswick, N.J.: Transaction Books, 1971), 273, quoted in Etzioni-Halevy, *The Knowledge Elite*, 26.

16. Etzioni-Halevy, *The Knowledge Elite*, 27.

17. Bell, "The New Class," 183.

CHAPTER 2

Power of a Third Kind: The Way It Works

Power of a third kind will be the defining element of the twenty-first century. Rapid changes in global electronic communications already leaves us breathless as we alter our daily lives just to keep up with the pace. For the world community, a minimally effective response requires that we strip away the confusion surrounding the Western concept of human power. It is high time we cast aside the entire "power is corrupt" and the "lust for power" rhetoric. Human power is there and is used because imposing one's vision on situations is a finite fact of being human. Western nations are already adapting their concept of power to fit opportunities inherent in power of a third kind. Their aggressive response has them far ahead in creating a world vision that, as one would expect, offers every advantage to the promotion of their national interests. If the entire globe accepts the Western definition, human power will be vested in the West.

These unprecedented conditions require, at minimum, equally unprecedented vision. Too often, however, non-Western intellectuals are so awe-struck by Western technology, resources, and affluent life-styles, they assume these "things" are the greatest power the West possesses. For much of this century such an assumption was appropriate. However, for the last three decades, narrow concentration on the "things" of power has made accurate political analysis and effective political response by non-Western nations nearly impossible. While Man has continued to create artificial ways of extending his ability, he has also discovered that the source of all this power was reflective thought and language. Because he is deeply in this third phase of Man's realization of his own power, it is natural that he would move toward "things" that would extend the power of his reflectivity and language.

Television, telecommunications, the Internet, and all such forms of technological extensions of thought, symbols, and images have been accepted and implemented throughout the globe. The speed with which this has happened is as startling as the wonders of the technology itself. The low-cost accessibility of televisions, computers, and radios by people throughout the world makes the received messages potentially available universally. Television has led the charge. After only a few decades in existence, it is as ubiquitous as nearly any other single invention since the telephone, indeed more so. In fact, there are more televisions worldwide than telephones.[1] Even when not actually in the homes of a majority of the individuals in cities, towns, and villages around the globe, very few human beings live beyond sight and sound of a television set. CNN, for example, has created a global audience in less than fifteen years, going from a largely domestic United States audience to 50 million viewers in Western Europe and 30 million viewers in the rest of the world.[2] Today, it is impossible to imagine any nation's elite that does not watch CNN or other Western programs. The incredible potential of this universal audience is an advertiser's dream.

These extensions of human consciousness offer new avenues for the use of the human power the technology imitates. When humans communicate, they do not move physical objects from one place to another. They are creating ways other human beings should imagine, envision, and interpret the world. When we talk about how entire nations can be brought to look at the world in ways advantageous to a certain communicator, we are talking about the essence of politics, the essence of communication, and the quintessence of human power. When we theorize about politics and power in this way, we move to the highest levels of human power and intellectual activity. Here, reflection on the innate power of human consciousness must give way to reflection on the efforts of people or nations to get other people to look upon a situation in a particular way. Intention-filled human beings make plans to enter that space in consciousness where a person finds the sources and inclinations to give meaning to the world in a certain way.

Human beings are never satisfied with order as an abstract concept; they want a particular kind of order. They want to control change and to give change directed impetus. Thus, these political intentions are just that, intended and thus never neutral. In fact, the beauty and the core logic of power in human action derives from this lack of neutrality. Intentionally instigated change, meant to achieve a certain kind of order, is so central to human action it is not surprising that human beings would want to control it. Getting others to accept one's concept of situated change is a major platform of power. The objective of the advertiser, the ideologist, and every great and farsighted leader is to have the ability to reach the everyday frameworks of people. They relish the opportunity to interpose their own meaning into events that fit within their guiding narratives.

Consider how political change can be made more readily acceptable when the framework for interpreting and judging "what's happening" is assumed by others as a universally applicable frame. This is power of a third kind, the dream of every hard-working ideologist. With such transcendent frames favorably connected to specific sets of events, simple manipulation is left far behind. The framework and the concept have a kind of one-to-one relationship. As a living thing, sustaining such a framework requires constant affirmation. Once a consensus is confirmed, the work of the ideologist as foreign policy planner would be to select and emphasize events that best use that culture-transcendent framework and keep it alive.

No political analyst from a developing nation can afford to see this as pure theory or academic speculation. If a developing nation had the power to establish interpretative frames that would positively comprehend its own needs and objectives, they would be irresponsible not to use such power. For over five hundred years, Western intellectuals have been working on the concept of liberal democracy as the most natural and thus the best form of government for all people. During that time, they have done everything possible to establish these concepts as the only way Man can advance, be happy, or find fulfillment. They have flown the banners of these terms on the Western side of the bi-polar struggle. They have successfully persuaded domestic constituencies to fund an awesome military machine to be used for Western strategic interests. Their experience and success in this long history of persuasion and manipulation is a critical component to their confidence in using power of a third kind.

The loss of the Western bi-polar rationale for exceptionality within a period of heightened multi-cultural diversity presents even more serious problems for leading Western nations. To create a transcendent and global framework able to justify Western actions, their foreign policy planners need access to non-Western elites, to their leaders, and to their constituencies. With such access, there is the possibility that a transcultural framework can be created. This will require a technical revolution in the way that foreign policy is made. Technology on its own will not be enough.

To use power of a third kind effectively, foreign policy will have to be wrapped around this technology. It has to mesh with the structure and rationale of the emerging media system. That is, whenever the leading Western nations have a need for exceptionality with regard to certain kinds of events, the West must feel certain that pro-Western, transcultural frameworks will be used by the media and by viewers to frame these events. However, the risks are high. Peoples' native, culturally grounded response to events does not disappear, even in the face of effective events framing. Their tendency to return to culturally connected political positions will, especially in times of crisis, always threaten to call culturally transcendent frames into question.

This chapter describes the early uses of power of a third kind and projects the shape of Western foreign policy in the next several decades. Here, the likely constraints and the advantages for maneuverability are briefly put forward. As will be seen, the Western nations' future as supra-national superpowers is not inevitable. Rather, like so much of our lives in this turbulent period, these political efforts are also works in progress. The world, in nearly every sphere of political action is, as it were, standing on one foot. Knowing where and when to put the other foot down is a subject of intense debate among Western foreign policy and commercial leadership. In the end, the primacy of intellectual effort will derive from a newly enhanced capacity to embrace and to activate the forces of subjective intention. All this effort will be tested in a massive attempt to impose a single vision of political assumption and process on a non-Western world certain to be sensitive to attempts at Western domination.

INVENTORY FOR A POST-INSULAR IDEOLOGICAL CONTEST

The end of the Cold War meant the end of a war that, for the primary combatants, was hotter ideologically than it was militarily. Despite the most expensive buildup of military hardware in the history of mankind, military conflict was largely carried out through third parties in venues outside the borders of the two powers. With the exception of Korea, Vietnam, and Afghanistan, "armed conflict," in superpower terms, was limited to low-level violence. Any threat in a developing country was assumed or enlarged upon, either by the Soviet Union or by the West.

Post–World War II intellectuals crafted a "good guy-bad guy" scenario for politicians and militarists to act out on the stage of developing nations. Socialism presented itself as having the greater concern for the masses with an economic system supposedly free from having to hang on the edge of survival. The combating narratives focused on portraying democratic capitalism as a facade of freedom and opportunity behind which full-time exploitation of the masses was being carried forward. Democratic capitalism presented its system as one of free enterprise and free choice where the "hidden hand of competition" and open political participation offered a life with economic affluence and free choice for anyone willing to work and to reach for it. Socialism was vilified as an attempt to control the world by taking away free choice and imprisoning people within the walls of communist ideology. A willingness to commit to one or the other carried with it access to protection, financial aid, technical assistance, and in certain cases, military assistance against domestic or border enemies.

In an incredibly abrupt fashion, this fifty-year epic ended in a victory of democracy over communism. The symbolic last skirmish of the Cold War may have been the tearing down of the Berlin Wall but the real ending was most felt in the developing world. Over this half a century, the politics and the economies of many developing nations have been shaped by this bi-polar struggle. Many of these countries had become dependent on the economic residue of the conflict. Both superpowers offered the incentive of aid and technical assistance; both distributed aid on the basis of their strategic military and economic interests. While both pushed their own mostly economic or ideologically self-serving form of development in the target country, they had no trouble shifting allegiances as interests dictated, featuring some countries on one side at one moment and then moving to the other side at another time.

To grasp the coming Western effort to adapt Cold War strategies and resources to a non–bi-polar and non-insular world, it is important to recognize that democracy and free market economies were always sold as "processes" on their own, distinctly apart from the anticipated or actual results. They were not presented as strategies for a better life but as narratives commanding belief in their purely symbolic magic. Underneath it all was the assumption that they would deliver a facsimile of

Western life. The hidden hand of capitalism had its supposed counterpart in democracy; the realization of the inherent efficacy of the two required only hard work and faith.

In essence, equal investment in the process was considered a "sufficient condition for realizing equal results."[3] Neither side felt the need to demonstrate that the competing processes actually resulted in promised or even any positive results. The world was fully predisposed to respond to a campaign where "democracy" or "socialism" as concepts could justify all sorts of action without actually delivering either one. This meant that, for half a century, the world was led to participate in a process where response to concepts was done without reference to fact. To understand this is to understand that the world also is predisposed to power of a third kind.

This is not to say that this persuasive effort was always cynical or entirely self-serving. Many on both sides were driven by a sincere belief in the oppressive exploitation inherent in democratic capitalism or the sinister destructiveness of communism. Whether cynical and self-serving or heartfelt and altruistic, such sentiments made little difference to developing countries. They certainly knew they were a part of an imposed process and they soon learned that they needed to be protected from either one or both of the superpowers.

This need for protection is the key to understanding the true dynamic of the Cold War and the underlying major assumption of the now developing post–Cold War rationale. It also is the key to understanding what really ended when that lethal play's final curtain came down in Berlin. To gain the support of domestic constituencies and the acquiescence of elites in foreign venues, both sides were committed to creating fear of their opposite. When the need for protection from the Soviet Union or from the United States was no longer a part of the international political rationale, the entire exchange strategy for access to resources, markets, and base sites had to be set aside for more timely and more credible justifications.

For developing countries, this absence of fear has become the transitional "empty space" left by the dramatic ending of the Cold War. The objective of the West is the same as before: unfettered low-cost, low-risk exceptional political advantage. The "how" of this new era for seeking access is the true story behind current events: Without the old bipolar threat with the Soviet Union as the "bad guy," how can Western nations use Cold War exceptionality to mobilize international and transnational intrusion into the economies and politics of the developing world?

A clear analysis of the constraints, advantages, and opportunities for bridging this "empty space" is the beginning point for understanding the future struggle for world dominance. This hiatus is wide and deep, a significant discontinuity in the entire raison d'être of global international transactions managed by the West for over fifty years. Filling this space began with the United States and the Clinton administration. Now all leading Western nations appear ready to work within a rationale that is still emerging. Bureaucratized intellectuals and their clients in government are reworking the first ideological and institutional planks of a bridge to a new justification for exceptionality. The political and economic resources of the entire planet already are being located and organized for its construction.

The key point in understanding the timing of this effort is the awareness that the bridge is not yet built and even the plans for its construction lie unfinished. Western intellectuals, in the media and government information agencies, do not have the leisure to explore the ramifications of current ideological scripts let alone develop entirely new ones. If the world would just stop until a new world order could be created reflecting Western problems, prospects, and intentions, all would be well. However, this is not the nature of the unceasing flow of change, especially in watershed transitions. Unlike the period following World War II, when most major industrial economies outside the United States were devastated, there is now no time to build a political or economic "Bretton Woods." In this sense, the G8 is a remarkable statement of the wavering potency of developed countries that need both a time and a place to meet outside of the arena, away from the accelerated pace of international competition.

The primary concern of developed nations is economic and the immediacy of their economic crisis makes the turbulent, rapidly altering currents of change even less forgiving. At minimum, the United States, Europe, and Japan require steady markets and steady resource supplies, internal economic stability, and the relatively quiescent support of most domestic polities. In particular, they need the concurrence of other countries in international institutions that it is better to work within the older Cold War terms of Western de facto dominance while the bridge is being constructed.

There are already international and transnational patterns in evidence that parallel the Western nations' immediate and long-term needs. Three patterns are emerging more or less simultaneously. Ultimately, these patterns converge into a foreign policy alternative significantly more advantageous to the West than all other available options.

First, the end of the Cold War resulted in the diminished importance of some aspects of military, institutional, and ideological resources previously integral to international transactions. Some of these resources have been completely set aside while others will be in evidence for the short term. However, certain approaches, resource uses, and positions recognizable as a central part of the Cold War strategy will continue to enjoy high priority.

Second, a massive restructuring of Western economies is occurring at the same time that the ideological rationale justifying Western hegemony is demanding an equally dramatic overhaul. The choice regarding which elements of the Cold War should be set aside and which kept is an utterly pragmatic question answered by the complicated flow of change—primarily economic—in the world today. To make sense of Western foreign policy strategies and responses in the present and to define a trend that will go far into the future, requires a sorting out of these movements and recombining them in meaningful ways.

Third, in less than three decades, Man has electronically extended human imaging and communication capacities to the extent that "real" time access to nearly every human being and certainly every decision maker has become a reality in nearly every human venue. The politics and the economy of an already well-organized structure of production and dissemination is a starting place for understanding the ways in which this technology can be used to catalyze a positive convergence of the first two trends. Any attempt to comprehend change in the contemporary international political scene without granting an equal place to electronic communications will result in a fatally partial analysis—not unlike describing the twentieth century without mentioning nuclear weapons.

In essence, the West has accomplished what its Cold War investment intended: to establish unchallenged military and political strength and, as a part of these strengths, to achieve de facto institutional control of international relationships. However, all this investment was not in the kind of infrastructure, primary or social, that makes for a good market position or competitive edge. Before the West could get off the Cold War train, Japan was pioneering the true meaning of "free market economy" on a different track. Eventually, the West has had to restructure its economy to maintain its competitive position. Even today, when

Asia is experiencing serious economic difficulties, the West is engaged in desperate efforts to maintain its competitive position in global markets.

Thus, the power is there but so are the constraints and the pressures of increasingly unsettled domestic constituencies and incrementally disenchanted developing countries. These Western nations are under attack from domestic groups dissatisfied with their standard of living and stressed by rising economic turmoil. It is as if these nations had invested their wealth for a post–Cold War retirement that turned out to be both inadequate and inappropriate. The assets for Western exceptionality are in inventory, but they do not quite fit the demands of this post–Cold War era.

GLOBAL MEDIA AS A SYSTEM, INSTRUMENT, AND PROCESS

For the West, identifying a new instrument of power that would satisfy its ever greater need for global exceptionality was an essential part of a successful post–Cold War strategy. What they found, after evaluating all the debits and credits of the power balance sheet, is the global ability to communicate in sight and sound from one central point to all corners of the planet. To make global communications just another set of inventions in human technological history is to ignore the quantum disjunction between this global accessibility and the access afforded by advances in say, transportation. As impressive as air and space travel are, they still require the physical presence of that weary traveler. Global communications went beyond the synthesis and extension of Nature when it created conditions for human communication that do not require human presence.

With this alteration, an entirely new dynamic came into being. Relative to human consciousness and to the immanent potential of the technologies themselves, we still are in the primitive, even embryonic, stages of realizing the impact and the potential of electronic communications. In the process of connecting—face to face—world-wide subjectivity, these technologies create a new force flowing into the way people look at the world and the way people think. They have opened unfamiliar venues with unexpected intensities. As with all technologies, new sources, new holders, and new structures of power are created. Today, man has new ways of imposing a different order, new ways of creating ever more human complexities.

Being a reflection of capacities within consciousness, electronic communications—television especially—is the least alien of all technological creations. It is not reactive like a shelter against the storm. It is not a replacement of physical capacity, like a backhoe is to an arm. It is an addition and expansion rather than an extension and a replacement. Like other less-powerful inventions, Man will use it, respond to it, build on it, and in so doing, will incrementally and dynamically change others and himself. This human-created reality, however, will simulate more and more the speed of the mind, itself. In these earliest days, television has already signaled that it has the capacity to fundamentally change the nature of human life and ways of living in every culture. Thus, despite denigration from all sides, television is likely the most human of all of Man's technology.

Except that one knows that the "it" on the screen is not another human being but only flashing images; there clearly is a difference between the shelf on which the television is placed and the images on the screen. Both are objects, but the television is packaged as a simulation of everyday conversation and interaction. The people on the set are not physically present but they are, if experienced, interacting with the viewer even if that transaction is carried forward in fantasy. The purpose in making these seemingly obvious comments is to make certain that television and its multiplying progeny are understood as much more politically and socially important than any other technological advance in the past.

MEDIA AS AN ACCESSIBLE SYSTEM FOR FOREIGN POLICY

The existence of electronic communications offers unprecedented opportunities for establishing international exceptionality. The outlines of its political economy are already discernible and have three essential elements. First, it is privatized and thus market dependent. Second, it is capital intensive for senders while easily and readily accessible to receivers. And, finally, because of its ability to shape and communicate images, messages, and events, it is open to the intentions of government policy makers.

To explicate the nature of this privatized system, there are five points that need developing. First, the media is made to appear neutral when it is no more neutral than any other entrepreneurial effort. Second, despite regulations to the contrary, all reporting is open to the corporate market pressures of media owners and their clients. Third, the media ratings system has no other intent than gathering information on specific consumer groups as a way of selling the media product to corporate advertisers. Fourth, the market-dependent business of electronic media creates a system open to government policy use without the need for direct government manipulation. Fifth, the same political economy that makes this system so internally tight makes the media product, as it is used by Western nations, more penetratingly powerful in developing countries.

One must begin with the commonsense understanding that the person who pays for the fuel in the tank has the most to say about where the car goes. This phrase suggests the most important factor affecting the use of this advanced communications technology and, more critically, shaping its impact: The enterprise of information production and dissemination is privatized. While such a statement may seem obvious to people accustomed to having every aspect of their lives commodified, developing countries may not be aware of the ramifications of such privatization. They may not be cognizant of the fact that the sale of its products does not end with the purchase transaction. They may not be aware that, despite its thoroughly entrepreneurial and profit-seeking structure, its ubiquitous presence in the home and in literally every venue of human living has given it a disarming quality of seeming neutrality. This apparent neutrality tends to mask the fact that it is owned by people engaged not in just reporting and entertaining but in selling.

When consumers are in a store and an item is presented for sale, there is a practiced caution based on the knowledge that the intention to make the sale is not entirely altruistic; in effect, there is a distance of disbelief between the buyer and seller. The television's presence in the home is a different experience. Events are reported without needing an immediate communicative response from the viewer. In an ambiance of neutrality, the viewer is told, "we are your eyes on the world." The technology is sold as though it were mute like any technology, an unbiased extension of the viewer's eyes and ears.

On top of this clear evidence of everyday commerce, the sacredness of "freedom of the press" has granted even more exceptionality to Western media. Even though both the media and its advertisers are corporations, the media process is treated quite specially. The entire structure suggests neutrality. This supposed neutrality resonates in the sender's oft repeated commitment to the viewer that events will be "reported *as they happen* from around the globe." The events happen, the viewer watches, and the only thing that is between the sender and receiver is this piece of furniture comfortably situated in the home. Repeating the creed of neutrality, the viewer is told to "relax while the world is brought to you."

No one trusts state-run media to have the ability to present matters without a political bias. Even government spokespersons are objects of widespread skepticism. The Western privatized media expects its viewers to depend on the reporters' service of "reading between the lines" and "getting the facts no matter where that takes us." The reporters themselves and the media corporations they represent are only doubted in the exception. Outside the media, politicians and literally everyone else are fair game for any kind of investigation or public castigation they might or might not deserve. When either politicians or corporations attack the media for even unlawful intrusion they are said to be just whining, or worse, trying to put pressure on a free, working press. When media products offend parents and frighten and shock children, the government only urges them to police themselves.

Most developing nations are aware of political polls being used to shape the message of would-be politicians, but many are not aware that the media ratings process is a twenty-four-hour polling effort. In the most remarkable market-testing effort, the responses of Western viewers are being checked, literally, at every moment. Too often, this testing is seen as a kind of personality contest. It is much more than that. The programs are not the only statistical facts being verified. The testing actually taps the way people living within Western culture interpret and give meaning to situations. Because the objective of the entire process is the choices of the consumer as viewer with regard to both the media and the advertisers' products, the process begins and ends with the consumer. That means Western consumers and, thus necessarily, Western culture set the context for the narratives and frameworks.

At this point, the political economy of power of a third kind and its relevance to non-Western countries shows itself in stark relief. Western governments do not need to intentionally create programs and broadcast news as an orchestrated effort to implant ideology. The reason conspiracy theorists have so much difficulty in proving government manipulation of the media is simple: Direct manipulation is not necessary. The Western media product is already filled with Western cultural assumptions or it would not be on the air. This is not reductionistic; it is simply an accurate statement describing the privatized system of images and messages produced and disseminated by and for private interests.

This observation throws light on the confusion felt by viewers in developing countries. Such comments as, "it is the media or the leadership, it is not the way the American or British or French people feel," simply do not take into account the circularity of program production. What viewers of Western television programming see finds its beginning and end within the cultural values and belief systems of Western consumers. The non-Western viewer of American programming, for example, gets a culturally packaged essence of American assumptions.

The United States exported to other countries more than three times the total amount of programming exported by the next three nations together. . . .

. . . In the entire Third World of 57 developing nations, 39 imported more than half of their television programming, and two-thirds of those 39 imported more than 60%.[4]

On the other hand, the American viewer sees nothing but Western programming. America "shares with Red China the distinction of having less hours (two percent) of its television time devoted to foreign programming than any other nation."[5] Thus, while powerful elites in developing countries are accessible by America, the American viewer, upon whose tastes and cultural predilections programming is created, receives almost no "outside" programming. This fact makes American programming creation responsive to an internal, largely protected, and entirely circular cultural system.

The general inability of developing countries to comprehend the role of media in the transnational projection of ideology derives largely from the Western assumption that the media is neutral. The reality is that the media cannot be neutral. At every moment, it is a hard sell backed by more investment in market testing than any other human activity. An ABC executive was very clear when he said, "the network is paying affiliates to carry network commercials, not programs. What we are is a distribution system for Procter & Gamble and other advertisers."[6] This awareness, however, does not always have the impact it should. As one study of prime-time news put it, "knowledge of who pays the bills can't be dispelled, even when it doesn't always rise to consciousness. Network executives internalize the desires of advertisers as a whole."[7] The media system responds to a very tight bottom line of time, profit, and loss. That this characterization also applies to the news was supported by former NBC News president Reuven Frank when he said: "News is a commodity; it's information retrieval. It's not a matter of better or worse; you sell it at the market price. It's like wheat."[8] The implication is that, if what you say cannot be funded with advertising, then the chances that it will be heard are minimal.

The media is an entirely accessible resource *because* of the fact rather than *despite* the fact that the production and dissemination of political and commercial information is a closed privatized system. At every moment, its consumer orientation and advertising sensibility make it an attractive resource for the mobilization of ideology without the need for conspiracies, political or otherwise. Its use is most available to America since both government and corporate advertisers depend on the same creedal frames and narratives. These, in turn, are certain to resonate in news, dramatic programs, and advertising presented in terms of a targeted, tested, and thoroughly known world of viewers. At the same time, these frames and narratives become the resources for every leading Western nation able to intervene in the flow of events or to initiate a more compatible international discourse.

Government ideologists do not have to enter these interpretative frames and narratives to make them compatible with their objectives; they already are compatible. The long-term integrity of the core narratives are protected by those government entities and those advertisers that depend on them for ratification and justification of actions. All this repetitive resonance is bonded by the certainty that Western consumers' commitment to these same frames and narratives will continue largely without critical thought.

Abetted by the emergence of electronic communications power, these same half-century-old frames and narratives are being affirmed, shaped, and reshaped for the "same" Western audience. Even when contradicted in terms of a single product, issue, or event, all are presented within and in terms of these cultural assumptions. Advertising presents the option of becoming Western or remaining "traditional" or "backward," of having democracy or no democracy, or having human rights or no human rights. These forced choices are the prime connection among foreign policy, advertising, and news and issues programming. If the campaign to establish a universal frame and a set of attractive narratives were beginning fresh without over a half-century of repetition, then the entire project would be almost as laughable as the narratives are transparently simplex. Because that is not the case, there is little reason for laughing.

One could argue that observations of everyday experience show human beings rarely taking on either/or judgments of their own role, positions, or attitudes. It is, in fact, difficult to imagine that otherwise intelligent people do not understand that an individual can decide to work *within* an institution at one moment yet act over *against* it at another. So, questions are asked, like, "Does the individual come before or after institutions?" Such either/or constructions do not allow one to inquire, "Does an individual have to come before the institution for him to be heroic, free, self-realized?" Or, "Isn't it possible for an individual to be both continuous and discontinuous from society?" Such arguments will not be heard by those people only capable of looking at the world through the mirror of their own culture.

This distortion of the human self and human culture comes from a long line of Western thought that assumes a human being will only rarely take a posture of distance from his culture and make individual decisions. This remarkable narrowing of human interpretative and imaginative power derives directly from the Western intellectuals' infatuation with systems that explain Man rather than Man's actions explaining and creating systems. When it is assumed that Western culture is *the* only universal culture, the binomial choice is only a rhetorical, not a real question. There actually is only one "true" choice.

Ironically, these either/or constructions—ostensibly meant to elevate the individual above institutions—end in placing the individual as viewer and consumer within the institutions of the market. He is told that without the media and the advertising presented on the media and paid for by corporations, his individual choice would be diminished. The Advertising Council's pitch to the viewer is, "Advertising: Your Right to Choose." This is on one hour and in the next, there is a United Nations' commercial with children telling viewers that they also have a "right to choose." Yes, in some cases and in terms of some cultures and some parents, they do. But, the theme of "right to choose" is really the elaborated cultural bias of Western liberal democratic political constructs placed within a narrative meant to affirm the Western political process. It is presented as an invitation to use that frame and an affirmation of that frame as a warrant for making that decision. This tactic is repeated endlessly: "AT&T offers 'the right choice'; Wendy's asserts that 'there is no better choice'; Pepsi is 'the choice of a new generation'; Taster's Choice is 'the choice for taste.'"[9] It is not surprising to find that the same advertising and policy elite polling the public's responses and interpretive frames would come up with the same advertising pitch. Finding them to be in conflict would be a more surprising disclosure.

Yet another major advertisement from the American Advertising Council is just as revealing. Here the viewer is told how much of his entertainment—from sports to concerts—would not be available if it were not for advertising. In another ad, the viewer is urged to consider how he could possibly make a choice without commercials. Both of these are surprisingly direct statements of the fact that the entire "info-tainment" project of television appears at the behest of the advertising industry and the dollars spent by corporations. It is a description of the actual state of affairs. This set of Advertising Council ads is a remarkable assertion of the power of corporations, media, and others to control experiential alternatives; real choices are only those that fit their privatized agenda.

"Choice" is the primary arena for advertising. A number of writers have pointed out that, since so many products are so similar, there is a need to distinguish one from another. In fact, advertisers claim that advertising adds value to the product through recognizable differentiation. But advertising adds more than value to products. When advertising invests a product "with powers it does not have in itself," it "'make[s] a fetish'" of a product.[10] This is an important characterization in coming to understand the way the concepts have been sold by ideologists during the Cold War and, particularly, how they will be sold in the next half-century.

Constituency and decision-maker choices are the crucial dynamic of democratic politics. It is in the area of choice that the promotion of products and concepts are quite similar. If you can take marginalized differences and characteristics in a product or a concept and add on values, you can upgrade them into fetishes. With careful manipulation of symbols, a car meant to get a person from one place to another is granted the ability, by itself, to establish the possessor as a successful person. Similarly, democracy goes from being just one form of government among many others to a badge of just and humane systems. Democratic governments become a fetish, where just being a democracy means that other democracies will not war with you or, that without it, a country cannot develop.

The right to choose becomes the right to use a single interpretative framework and only those choices implicated by that framework. It is not surprising that, after three decades of melded product and concept projection to the citizen as consumer, Americans say, "I'm sorry, I can't buy that" when talking about political issues. That these countless, dramatized choice situations would result in quite undifferentiated roles as citizens and as consumers is an expected and a predictable result. Just as predictable is the idea that consumer events and political events would become blended into the syntax of choosing.[11]

This is where the Western nations can see some return on their investment in the promotion of democracy during the Cold War, where concepts were sold in a massive and extremely expensive advertising program. Pressure was put on every country to "make a choice" between "our" concept or someone else's. Every nation was forced at one time or another to lay down everything from lives to resources in the name of this or that concept, all in order to gain the acceptance of one of the bi-polar competitors. These concepts were multiplied and refined year after year and are still being manufactured, reshaped, and sold today. Like a consumer's choice, a citizen's choice was limited to what was produced; in this case, by just two bi-polar producers. The choice was "free" only to the extent of the alternative "products" these two sources offered. The job of ideologists was to package and make an attractive fetish of their own particular alternative.

Thus, the selling of value-added commodities and concepts is derived from similar systems responding to a similar syntax, economy, and politics. These systems operate within the same logic, tuned and manipulated by the same professional personnel. They are operationally dependent on the responses of consumers to the market, the same middle-class and upper-middle-class Western consumers who have been the targets of these systems for over half a century.

THE VIEWER AS CONSUMER AND CITIZEN

Because the viewer is approached in the singular role of consumer and the West has become the archetypal haven of such consumption, the global viewer will be communicated with less in terms of his culture than in terms of his cultural aspirations as a consumer. He is not being asked to act the role of citizen or make citizen choices. Instead, he is being asked to "consume" culturally loaded, politically relevant Western frameworks and narratives. At some point, the citizen/consumer is asked to choose what advertising professionals call a "global brand" of political concepts.

Products carry the capacity to catalyze existing social meanings; thus, the connection between the terms "packing" and "packaging."[12]

The package and the product have use functions but they also include social, motivational, and identity functions the advertiser wants to tap. In this very important sense, then, "media *are* agencies of mediation, that in reporting events they also propose certain frameworks for the interpretation of those events, moulding or structuring our consciousness in ways that are socially and politically consequential."[13] Thus, while required by law to be politically neutral, the last Director General of the BBC, Sir Charles Curran, said that the network was "'biased in favour of parliamentary democracy.'"[14]

Billions of dollars are spent in finding and defining these frameworks so that, no matter what the product, the "packaging" will interest and, hopefully, motivate the consumer. Consumers are not passive in this process. They identify the social importance of purchasing the product and the importance of the act of purchasing to their own status and sense of self-worth. They also are aware of the importance of the source of the product. Consumers worldwide identify with the unchallenged status of a few super-successful, super-producing, and super-consuming Western nations. Whether fiction or reality, the developing world's idea of a consumer's "good life" is to live and buy in the West. In this way, to developing-nation consumers, "buying American"—or British or French—means more than just purchasing products. These acts of consumption are acts that affirm the desirability of "buying into" the Western experience.

Even when there is the potential for marginal conflict, viewer involvement as a consumer of fetishized products and concepts eases their resistance to transcending their assumptions as citizens. Such consumption has already become one of the most transcultural and utterly "global" of all modern experiences. The predisposition toward global concepts is created by the values, frames, and narratives in the packaging of products. In political matters, this is the fundamental basis for creating Western global brands of political choice and process.

Just experiencing the programs and advertised products will not lead, on its own, to major cultural change. Such a naïve view of the role and impact of the media does more to underestimate than overstate its power. When it is reported by advertisers that they no longer need to adapt their message to China or Thailand, this is not to say that the people in these countries think Western and have generally dispatched their traditional cultural beliefs. Rather, at this stage, they have simply become Western consumers on their way to becoming global Western citizens. From a Western foreign policy perspective, they have become accessible and susceptible to ideological mobilization through their participation as consumers of media and manufactured products. They are, in the jargon of the electronic media, "on-line" and predisposed to imaginatively and actively participate in the narratives and frameworks presented to them.

The establishment of a "global brand" of Western political culture will not happen in a single day, if at all. But establishing overarching political concepts as active judgmental frames may not be as difficult to achieve as one might imagine. Use of power of a third kind marks the beginning of an ideological effort never before experienced by human beings. The timelines are not known, but what is known is that the process for creating a universal Western culture is becoming ever more apparent and the potential for success more believable than it was less than three decades ago. There is clear evidence that consumers, worldwide, are becoming accustomed to using Western frameworks and narratives tied together with fetishized symbols.

Among intellectuals, there is a tendency to overemphasize the difficulty of establishing these frameworks and their narratives. This is because they see persuasion as a space-specific—people-facing-people—experience. They fail to recognize that the "spaceless" experience of electronically transmitted communication is more than marginally different. Beyond the viewers' identity of themselves as consumers and their identification with an absent audience of Western consumers, there is the generic experience of their participation in the electronic communication process. The media's presence in the "here" and its capacity to represent the "there" of the entire world is at least as powerful as perceptions in an instance of one-to-one communication in shared physical space. Telephone communications more nearly approach normal physical, space-dependent interactions than does television. With the latter, the communication offers little opportunity for interactive participation by the consumer/viewer. He is a spectator even more separate from the actors and speakers than at a play or a sporting event. The real applause is not heard until the ratings come out or until products are sold.

Yet the absent audience is there and the viewer is aware of its presence. When the viewer observes the news in his home, he knows that this same report is being experienced by tens of millions of people, many of them simultaneously witnessing the same events he is seeing and hearing. These absent millions are "consuming"—choosing to watch—at the same time he is watching but not in the same place. He is, in effect, a member of a global electronic fantasy culture, a culture without any necessary connection to his own. He can participate in this culture without experiencing any conflictual response to his local cultural themes and assumptions.

In the viewer's everyday life, space and time come together in the physical presence of the people doing the communicating. In such everyday situations, just the act of granting one's attention is an expression and a resource for the exertion of power. The modernity of television "tears space away from place by fostering relations between 'absent' others."[15] In this sense, the television relationship is an invitation—through the supposed neutrality of television technology—to be an unquestioning, mute part of an assumed consensus with other viewers. This consensus is verified by the "neutral" commentator reporting the news.

As long as the viewer participates in the one-sided listener/viewer role, he is, at the very least, transported into that absent audience via the vehicle of the credibility he accords the media itself. In simple terms: Despite the fact that no one else in the absent audience has the opportunity to question the news narrative either, the viewer is actually saying, "If this were not the case, they wouldn't say it in front of so many people." In this way, he becomes a vicarious part of the broadcast narrative through the credibility he grants to the "neutral" media. Because the values and norms that guide the narrative are necessarily Western, he is chronically involved as a viewer granting that narrative and its values similar levels of credibility and objectivity.

The persistence of these narratives are most notable in the way they shape and distort the supposed objectivity of reporters. Despite the appearance of televised news programs "as raw, unprocessed reality; as the world narrating itself,"[16] it is no less editorializing as the opinion section in local newspapers. Studies indicate that "news stories ultimately us[e] actual events to retell generic stories with broad cultural themes. Thus, reporters subconsciously fit information into story patterns that reinforce broad cultural paradigms or myths."[17] This means that "the consensual aspects of news reporting, both among journalists and sources, make it almost impossible to derail a narrative once it is begun."[18]

The narrative becomes the chronically communicated framework for organizing the events reported. It becomes a part of the discourse of the viewer. Even when he has widely different opinions about the particularities of individual events, he still uses the same worn narratives to comprehend a variety of similar and dissimilar events. The reporters' unconscious use of the narrative lies under the cloak of neutrality and objectivity. The framework survives long after the events themselves are forgotten. Once the narrative frame is established in the discourse of viewers, it is a resource for the ideologists. This becomes particularly significant if that ideologist's country has the power to intrude into and shape the agenda of on-going events in ways that occasion the use and affirmation of that narrative.

A critical aspect of this process is the way in which such reporting is structured within the media. Basically, news can be reported thematically by presenting issues in a "general or abstract context." Or, the news can be presented episodically, in terms of "concrete instances or specific events."[19] The political economy of market-directed news programming rarely allows for in-depth analysis because the networks simply cannot afford it. "In fact, television news coverage of political issues is heavily episodic. Two-thirds of all stories on poverty broadcast between 1980 and 1986 concerned a particular poor person. Similarly, of the nearly two thousand stories on terrorism, 74 percent consisted of 'live' reports of some specific terrorist act, group, victim, or event while 26 percent consisted of reports that discussed terrorism as a general political problem."[20] The creation of the news magazine, a permutation on the "nightly news," offered viewers even more "narrative" in an even more episodic form.

Rather than analysis, the viewer is given one picture after another, edited to make it all into a story, a narrative that resonates with the reporter's assumptions and the producers' market awareness. In fact, the "up-to-the-minute information . . . tends to devalue events by making them appear either as unforeseeable happenings or as inescapable proof of the truth of ideological constructs."[21] In this way, terrorist or worker strikes, for example, are presented in much the same fashion: They are unfortunate breaks in the "normal" pattern of safety and certainty in the Western status quo world.

Framed by and within the tight narratives of Western cultural responses, the events come already framed. Lacking any analysis of their particular context and causes, events can then serve the purpose of reiterating that narrative. Because of this, in a world of episodically televised news, the only real place for government, and to some extent business, is in the direct intervention and manipulation not of the themes or the information, but of the events themselves.

Just as episodic but with even less time than a news story, the commercials interspersed between presented events are themselves repetitions of the same narratives. Advertising executives are an elite group, functioning within a tightly interconnected social class—a condition comparable to the foreign policy and journalistic elites.[22] Like the reporter, the commercial-creating professional must make life large and hyper-real, but he must do it all in seconds, not minutes. There is no time for thematic exploration. Advertisements must "refer not only to things and situations but also to ways of seeing and interpreting them."[23] The narrative underpinnings of the "pitch" must be immediately recognizable and interesting enough to hold back the power of the remote channel changer.

Advertising is best seen as an activity that does not directly change attitudes or assumptions. Indigenous frames are not to be confronted, only located, comprehended, and reached. This results in the reinforcement of an already existing understanding held by the largely American middle-class to upper-middle-class viewer. Again, viewers will give meaning to experienced situations from their collection of such interpretative frames. Advertisers never make the mistake of trying to create or alter assumptions.

Advertisers purchase the watching time of targeted viewers.[24] Governments can only purchase watching time by creating or shaping or intervening in events in ways that will, in the view of media and their experience with the consumers, interest the viewing audience. In essence, media is saying to governments: "We sell audience viewing time; if you make yourself interesting enough and important enough, relative to other event options for garnering audience viewing time, then we will give you the time." Governments know that this is the true meaning of objectivity: Media will be objective and tell both sides of the story to the extent that both sides are interesting enough and cost efficient enough to capture enough viewing time to sell next week's advertising. Thus governments' relationships to media moves further and further from a focus on the dissemination of "objective" information to identifying and structuring events that position them to their best advantage.

"PLUGGING IN" TO FOREIGN POLICY

Global viewers are a growing resource for power, and they will be used as such. The future shape of Western foreign policy regarding non-Western countries will feature an effort toward the integration of media-projected information pitched toward consumers as purchasers of products and as citizens making political choices. In these terms, then, the task of government information policy is to make the events equally "predictable" in the sense that the reporting of the events accurately follows a narrative likely to justify Western demands for exceptionality.

This is no small challenge. It is less of a challenge, however, when one understands that countless episodic events are not just an unrelated chaos of images. There is a pattern, a pattern responsive to the political economy of its extensive privatization and the cultural narratives of those people who own and work for the media. That pattern, once known, becomes a resource filled with as much opportunity for the ideologist as for the advertiser. With access to billions of viewers, the media product becomes an unprecedented foreign policy resource as interpretative frames and narratives are constantly repeated twenty-four hours a day in news, drama, and commercials. These frames and narratives are the primary resource for the use and realization of power of a third kind.

The entire privatized system is ready for foreign policy intellectuals to "plug into." The final piece to the puzzle of power lies in the heightened concern for safety entailed in living in the "risk society."[25] Simply put, researchers are becoming aware of a fear response deriving from the "globalization of risk."[26] This is the global projection of events, which, less than three decades ago, might not have been known and certainly would not have been experienced in anything like real time. Despite warnings that "the following scenes may be too unpleasant for sensitive viewers or small children," news reporting carries the viewer into "real-life" dramas. Then, seconds later, the viewer is "dropped" back into his familiar, yet now strangely altered, surroundings.

The viewer as consumer in developed and developing countries is given every reason to feel vulnerable in a world that is less and less risk free. With households accustomed to having their sets on nearly seven hours a day,[27] it is not surprising to find research reporting that "heavy viewing tends to bring people of otherwise divergent political views into the mainstream construction of reality portrayed by television."[28] All this repetitive experience creates a "knowledgeable" consumer.

The real power of transnational electronic communications begins to show itself when the impact of Western products, Western culture, Western values, and Western military combine with global institutional concurrence that Western nations are the world leaders and protectors.

All this is then topped off with the equally exciting drama of these nations as the champions of "risk relief" for all countries. The promise of risk relief becomes the stated justification for controversial policies. For example, United States Secretary of State Madeleine Albright, pressed to justify the expansion of NATO, stated that the objective was not to confront the Soviet Union but that expansion is necessary to "maintain stability."[29]

Take sovereignty, for example. It is the right accorded to all nations, by the world community, to make choices about their own political, economic, military, and cultural alternatives without intrusion from the outside. Traditionally, this is a right that has wide consensus throughout the world. As stated by the World Court in 1966, the consensus is quite clear that "the state 'is subject to no other state, and has full and exclusive powers within its jurisdiction.'"[30] But in our twenty-first century global village, treatment of any nation's citizens will—and must—have the full scrutiny of other nations to prevent or at least minimize human suffering under oppression. However, this scrutiny by other nations cannot be allowed to totally invalidate the sovereignty of a nation, lest it be abused for the political purposes of one nation over another. Sovereignty is the unnamed underpinning for the critical rights debates of today: human rights, environmental rights, women's rights, habitat rights, and any rights that non-Western cultures may not have even heard of.

Western intellectual circles are in search of a policy that would create a "reconstituted sovereignty" to replace the nation-state they see as outdated in a modern and a "post-modern" world. When a nation-state signs one of the several human rights treaties that directly or indirectly agrees to outside interventions for whatever justification, that state must realize it is participating in the redefining of sovereignty. This effort to establish human rights as a justification for intervention is gathering force. As recently as 1992, the Carnegie Endowment for International Peace hailed "a 'new principle of international relations'—namely, that respect for a nation's sovereignty was no longer justified if it was violating human rights on a large scale, or if it otherwise presented what the report called a 'humanitarian crisis.'"[31]

A sort of forced choice is currently being presented. That is, if we are to achieve rights for the individual, especially human rights, we must become a global community without the petty tyrannies and traditional chauvinism of so many separate nations. The subtext is always there: If we cannot uproot these national boundaries, we must find an internationally acceptable way to set aside sovereignty using individual rights, or democratic process, or "habitat," or any other acceptable rationale. The new United Nations' Secretary General, Kofi Annan of Ghana, reflected this new principle of international relations when he said, within weeks of assuming his duties, that "we cannot permit nations to hide behind the walls of sovereignty on human rights."[32]

The Secretary General is correct if first there is a clear global consensus on the meaning of "human rights," "religious freedoms," or "environmental rights." Most likely, when the world's nations came together to form this consensus there would be no disagreement on the general principles. The real challenge would be in the details, with each culture debating these rights from within their own historical context—definitely a difficult and exhausting undertaking. Without this process, however, the only alternative is the promotion of one set of rights by the West and its imposition through forced choices. The promotion of these rights would not be the objective in and of itself and would be seen as a vehicle for advancing Western political interests. This will cause rage in non-Western nations and, ultimately, undermine the attractiveness of these rights.

The same is true in the promotion of democracy. Lacking the old bipolar ideology, there is no option during the present transition but to make "democracy" the primary vehicle for maintaining Western exceptionality. In the coming Western exceptionality campaign, democracy will be the defining concept for who is "right" and who is "wrong." The aspiration to be a democratic country will not be as much the determining factor as will be the fear of being a "rogue" nation without any or enough democracy.

The prime foreign policy objective is to achieve a universal consensus among non-Western elites and middle classes that Western liberal democracy is an inherently human and, thus, an innately neutral process. As such, actions taken to protect that neutral process also would be neutral, altruistic, and deserving of exceptionality from the rules binding the rest of the international community. This exceptionality would render "acceptable" certain violations of sovereignty and would help to justify demands for special advantages in supposedly free markets.

Achieving this level of presumption would not be possible without the full integration of electronic media into foreign policy or, it is better to say, without the integration of foreign policy within the grammar of a fully systematized media structure. As the system for production, shaping, and projection of global media programming evolves, key decisions are being made that have already come to characterize and control the bulk of the activity to be brought forward into the future. As each of these decisions ends in structures, a political economy forms around them, a political economy that is largely transparent and mostly predictable.

If ten plus years is intermediate term, and twenty to thirty years is long term, a singular question faces Western leadership: How do they achieve and maintain exceptional access to resources and markets in the intermediate term without a recognizable enemy? And what kind of bridge would have to be built to maintain such exceptional access in the longer term?

The answer to these questions lies in a cold-eyed analysis of the constraints that currently mitigate the overwhelming power of developed Western nations. In the intermediate term, they will have to create an enemy from whom developing nations need protection. In the longer term, they will need a global ideological justification for Western exceptionality without so much dependence on the negative actions of any clear enemy or on costly Cold War political, military, and economic exchanges.

If, in this age of transnational vulnerability, a controller of electronic communications can reach people in mental space without having to go in-country or to adapt to in-country assumptions, the mobilization of ideology becomes much more cost effective and efficient in establishing universal ethnocentric frames.[33] Acceptance of this exceptionality, without censure or only negligible censure, is the goal. In such mobilizing efforts, the ideologist is not searching for full point-for-point belief. Rather, this new wave foreign policy takes its lessons from the pragmatics of advertising: Can an event activate a certain frame of perception that harbors little or no conflict among the world's cultures; and will that frame cause the event to be perceived in a proscribed and positive way?

Ideology must not be seen in the older treatise or textual sense, a great opus of carefully articulated thought to be debated among the intellectual elite. With power of a third kind, we are dealing with the kind of street corner ideology Aristotle talked about in *Rhetoric*. Filled with the push and pull of elite egos, special interests, and conflicting agendas, it is more the work of intellectuals. It is open-ended, ambiguous, overtly simplistic, and slightly overstated.

As these lines are being written, the realists, the neo-realists, and the critical foreign policy theorists are in an intense dialogue over the direction and strategy of Western foreign policy. However, resolution is in sight to the point that the discourse and the symbols used are beginning to appear repetitive. As the "end of history" and the "end of the Cold War" lose their place and their credibility as analytic points of departure, new plays on very old concepts have begun to emerge and, in the mercurial manner of policy making, to gather power. The framework that will attend the "world brand" for a global justification of policy is clearly in the making.

The achievement of these intermediate and long-term goals are incredibly challenging for Western nations. That they have amassed a stunning amount of military, economic, institutional, and ideological power is beyond question. Equally unarguable is the avowed intention to use that power to sustain leadership. When power of a third kind is added to this stockpile, the bridge to unfettered access will have been built.

For non-Western nations, this will be an equally challenging time. If this transnational strategy to attain unrestrained and uncontested access is not grasped in all its sophistication, the West will successfully achieve an exceptionality over most questions of sovereignty. The old rules of fifty years' lineage were largely written to fit the West during different times. Their need for a different market posture and competitive position requires substantial exceptionality from these rules. This exceptionality will be marked by impatience with any demand that the actions of Western nations have reciprocity, that they actually do what they require everyone else to do.

To this point our analysis has carried us through a representation of emerging strategies likely to be used within this new power of a third kind. Having done so, does this analysis make Western foreign policy actions comprehensible, and can they be predicted with enough clarity to allow a timely response? When these questions are answered positively, non-Western nations can move away from the footless posturing of spectators to the proactive role of participants in decisions that will shape their countries' futures.

NOTES

1. *Information Please Almanac*, 49th ed. (Boston: Houghton Mifflin Company, 1996), 564.

2. "Some Limits on the Global Village," *New York Times*, 4 May 1994, sec. A, p. 12, late New York edition.

3. Richard J. Ellis, "Rival Visions of Equality in American Political Culture," *The Review of Politics* 54 (Spring 1992): 255. For the way in which democracy and capitalism are presented in tandem within the Western concept of freedom, see Jochen Hippler, "Democratisation of the Third World After the End of the Cold War," in *The Democratisation of Disempowerment: The Problem of Democracy in the Third World*, ed. Jochen Hippler, Transnational Institute Series (London: Pluto Press, 1995), 18.

4. James A. Brown, *Television "Critical Viewing Skills" Education: Major Media Literacy Projects in the United States and Selected Countries* (Hillsdale, N. J.: Lawrence Erlbaum Associates, Publishers, 1991), 20.

5. Richard Collins, *Culture, Communication, and National Identity: The Case of Canadian Television* (Toronto, Ont.: University of Toronto Press, 1990), 14, quoting Sandra Gathercole, "The Best Film Policy this Country Never Had," in *Take Two*, ed. S. Feldman (Toronto: Irwin, 1984), 41.

6. William Hoynes, *Public Television for Sale: Media, the Market, and the Public Sphere* (Boulder, Colo.: Westview Press, 1994), 33, quoting Ken Auletta, *Three Blind Mice: How the TV Networks Lost Their Way* (New York: Random House, 1991), 301.

7. Hoynes, *Public Television for Sale*, 30, quoting Todd Gitlin, *Inside Prime Time* (New York: Pantheon, 1985), 253.

8. Lewis A. Friedland, *Covering the World: International Television News Services*, Perspectives on the News Series (New York: Twentieth Century Fund, Inc., 1992), 39, quoting Reuven Frank, interview with Friedland, 6 February 1992.

9. James B. Twitchell, " 'And Now a Word From Our Sponsor,' " *The Wilson Quarterly* 20 (Summer 1996): 71.

10. Sut Jhally, *The Codes of Advertising: Fetishism and the Political Economy of Meaning in the Consumer Society* (New York: St. Martin's Press, 1987), 28.

11. For a discussion of the viewer as citizen, see Graham Murdock and Peter Golding, "Information Poverty and Political Inequality: Citizenship in the Age of Privatized Communications," *Journal of Communication* 39 (Summer 1989): 180–95. For the role of the consumer and "choosing," see Arjun Appadurai, "Disjuncture and Difference in the Global Cultural Economy," in *Global Culture: Nationalism, Globalization and Modernity*, ed. Mike Featherstone, A *Theory, Culture & Society* Special Issue (London: SAGE Publications, 1990), 307.

12. Terence H. Qualter, *Advertising and Democracy in the Mass Age* (New York: St. Martin's Press, 1991), 48.

13. Tony Bennett, "Media, 'Reality', Signification," in *Culture, Society and the Media*, eds. Michael Gurevitch, Tony Bennett, James Curran, and Janet Woollacott (London: Methuen, 1982), 288.

14. *Ibid.*, 289, quoting Stuart Hall, I. Connell, and L. Curti, "The 'Unity' of Current Affairs Television," *Working Papers in Cultural Studies* 9 (1976): 57.

15. Anthony Giddens, *The Consequences of Modernity* (Cambridge, UK: Polity, 1990), 18, quoted in Shaun Moores, "Media, Modernity, and Lived Experience," *Journal of Communication Inquiry* 19 (Spring 1995): 7.

16. Bennett, "Media, 'Reality', Signification," 303.

17. Thomas Roach, "Competing News Narratives, Consensus, and World Power," in *The U.S. Media and the Middle East: Image and Perception*, ed. Yahya R. Kamalipour, Contributions to the Study of Mass Media and Communications Number 46 (Westport, Conn.: Greenwood Press, 1995), 28, quoting S. Elizabeth Bird and Robert W. Dardenne, "Myth, Chronicle, and Story: Exploring the Narrative Qualities of News," in *Media, Myths, and Narratives: Television and the Press*, ed. I. W. Carey (Newbury Park, Calif.: Sage Publications, 1988), 70–72.

18. Roach, "Competing News Narratives," 29.

19. Shanto Iyengar and Adam Simon, "News Coverage of the Gulf Crisis and Public Opinion: A Study of Agenda-Setting, Priming, and Framing," in *Taken By Storm: The Media, Public Opinion, and U.S. Foreign Policy in the Gulf War*, eds. W. Lance Bennett and David L. Paletz, American Politics and Political Economy Series (Chicago: The University of Chicago Press, 1994), 171.

20. Ibid., 171–72.

21. Marie-Christine Leps, "Empowerment Through Information: A Discursive Critique," *Cultural Critique* 31 (Fall 1995): 182.

22. Chiara Giaccardi, "Television Advertising and the Representation of Social Reality: A Comparative Study," *Theory, Culture & Society* 12 (February 1995): 111.

23. Ibid., 114.

24. Jhally, *The Codes of Advertising*, 72.

25. Moores, "Media, Modernity, and Lived Experience," 9, referencing Anthony Giddens' use of Ulrich Beck's phrase, "risk society" in Ulrich Beck, *Risk Society: Towards a New Modernity* (London: Sage Publications, 1992).

26. Anthony Giddens, *The Consequences of Modernity*, 124, quoted in Moores, "Media, Modernity, and Lived Experience," 10.

27. Hoynes, *Public Television for Sale*, 26.

28. Robert A. White, "Mass Communication and Culture: Transition to a New Paradigm," *Journal of Communication* 33 (Summer 1983): 287, referring to the Cultural Indicators Project of George Gerbner and associates at the Annenberg School of Communications, University of Pennsylvania, as presented in George Gerbner, Larry Gross, Michael Morgan, and Nancy Signorielli, "Charting the Mainstream: Television's Contributions to Political Orientations," *Journal of Communication* 32 (Spring 1982): 100–127.

29. Madeleine Albright, *CNN WorldNews*, 23 February 1997.

30. This classical definition of sovereignty is given by the World Court in the Wimbledon case, as cited in Stanley Hoffmann, "International Systems and International Law," in *The Strategy of World Order*, vol. 2, *International Law*, eds. Richard A. Falk and Saul H. Mendlovitz (New York: World Law Fund, 1966), 164, quoted in Kathryn Sikkink, "Human Rights, Principled Issue-Networks, and Sovereignty in Latin America," *International Organization* 47 (Summer 1993): 413.

31. Peter W. Rodman, *More Precious than Peace: The Cold War and the Struggle for the Third World* (New York: Charles Scribner's Sons, 1994), 545.

32. Kofi Annan, *CNN WorldNews*, 1996.

33. For a definition of ideology as a movement that makes perspectives appear natural or inevitable, see Stuart Hall, "The Rediscovery of 'Ideology': Return of the Repressed in Media Studies," in *Culture, Society and Media*, edited by Michael Gurevitch, Tony Bennett, and Janet Woollacott (London: Methuen, 1982), 65.

CHAPTER 3

First Uses of Power of
a Third Kind

For the West, the historic transition from the Cold War to the dream of "Pax Occidental" will require a dramatic transition from the assumption of inviolable national sovereignty to the dream of a global village where liberal Western concepts are crowned universal. Attaining the global village and the hegemony it offers will require a foreign policy as visionary in its altruism as it must be realistic in its strategic pragmatism. Getting the entire world to move to a community of nations without borders will require the widespread assumption that there are rights to be acquired, standards to be met, and a perfection to be reached that is utterly Western. There is another corollary assumption that would have to gain an equally tight consensus: Western nations must be allowed the widest possible range of exceptionality to protect democratic states from non-democratic ones.

This ideological agenda is a daunting one, but power of a third kind is simply too promising in its effect and too limited in risk and cost to set aside. This is especially the case when all Western governments are facing strong external market competition and a desperate need to re-structure internal economies. Western intellectual elites within the foreign policy establishment have already begun to face this challenge. This is especially true in the United States under Presidents Bush and Clinton. The efforts are not in the least conspiratorial. In fact, within and outside the government, elite foreign policy professionals have publicly announced their readiness to use their relative power advantages to make their culture and their politics globally universal. At least publicly, the current American administration is indicating a high level of optimism for success. President Bill Clinton, in February 1993:

> [T]he new world toward which we are moving actually favors us. We are better equipped than any other people on Earth by reason of our history, our culture, and our disposition, to change, to lead, and to prosper. . . .
>
> Look at the way our culture has merged technology and values. This is an expressive land that produced CNN and MTV.[1]

Neither the victories and defeats of American intentions, nor the sense of mission and their guiding constructs has changed. The hundred-year perception of America as the carrier and defender of Western culture has consolidated around the identity of the United States as a country destined to be a supra-national moral authority. In the minds of most American elites, the United States success in communications technology has, almost by itself, seemed to confirm that mission and destiny. To most American intellectuals, it seems entirely natural that a technology would be developed in America that would be the primary vehicle for broadcasting the seeds of democracy throughout the earth. Clinton's Deputy Secretary of State Strobe Talbott was explicit when speaking before the Carnegie Endowment for International Peace in 1996:

> Today, there is, around the globe, more grass-roots support for democracy than at any other time in human history. In part, this is because of modern communications. The Soviet communist system collapsed not just because it was contained by military power but also because it was penetrated and subverted by information and ideas. Even the most heavily fortified borders became increasingly permeable first to radio, then to television, and eventually to the interactive influences of telefax and e-mail.[2]

This technological optimism blends with America's messianic vision to confirm that it is right and good that America is the only remaining superpower. On the surface, the logic is quite clear and, in varying degrees, is assumed by the leading industrial countries that make up the Group of Eight (G8). Developed Western nations are, in fact, exceptional in their accomplishments, so why shouldn't they be granted exceptionality? Reciprocity is an option only for equals; Western nations are without any true equals. Foreign policy intellectuals perceive that it is the burden of Western nations to establish the standards and the parameters of global action and interaction for all other nations.

Besides material and institutional power, Western Europe and America are strongly identified with democracy. They have paid for that association with over fifty years of serious material and human investment. In the international arena and in their own domestic perceptions, a few Western nations hold copyright to the term "democracy." In these days following the Cold War, "democracy" and all its cluster of political "rights" and "freedom" terms are ready to be enlisted in confronting a weakening market position. In the logic of power and international discourse, it is less than the turn of a linguistic hand to urge the world to assume that the problem of markets can be solved if, like a free, democratic political process, they, too, were free.

Thus, Western intellectuals have created a new symbolic architecture of discourse. The result is a new foreign policy campaign of "market democracy." This campaign begins with an already educated, if not entirely receptive, audience. For politicians desperately looking for a much needed international edge, market democracy offers a very appealing rhetoric. That a Western consensus has developed out of this American intellectual initiative is apparent from an analysis of the international discourse. In a single day, when commenting on an event or issue, American, British, and French foreign ministers will use the same terms to frame and justify their decisions. In this discourse, all nations are urged to "get into" the democratic process and free markets. Separating culture, as it does, from political choice, political process, and political action, this program trivializes the nature and impact of the choices to be made. No consideration is given to external pressures or internal deficiencies that might actually block certain nations from getting into one or the other of these two panaceas.

Underlying this discourse is the strategy of assuming that everyone shares the Western nations' problems, if not on the same scale and with the same intensity. Making everyone else's problems the same as one's own allows the opportunity to point to the same enemy and the same solution. Thus the West can use the parallel assumptions that "free" markets are essential to rights protecting democracies and that "free" democratic process is essential to viable economies. "Political and economic diplomacy are indivisible," said Clinton's former Secretary of

State Warren Christopher. For this administration, gone are the "high politics" of balance-of-power competition and the "low politics" of economics[3]; gone is "sphere of influence" foreign policy and gone is "containment." Rather, in these early days of power of a third kind, the Clinton administration's focus is on a policy of "enlargement": more robust economies, more democratic nations, more free trade, more human rights, more sustainable development, more freedom. Thus, while politics and economics are "indivisible," they consider politics and culture quite divisible because it is culture that is thought to get in the way of the global trend toward "freedom."

GIVING MAGIC TO EVERYDAY TERMS

These positions are not entirely original nor are they without precedent in Western foreign policy. However, the emphasis and the "mix" are different. They do fit the creedal pattern of missionary zeal and liberal democratic ideas used in the past to persuade American and European constituencies to support foreign involvement. The difference lies in the newly realized ability to use power of a third kind to establish culturally transcendent global referents for "democracy," "human rights," and "free markets," and to elevate them to a level of almost supernatural status. American foreign policy analyst Francis Fukuyama reflects this prevailing sentiment when he says, "The fundamental impulse toward liberal democracy springs from a noneconomic desire for 'recognition.' The relationship between economic modernization and democracy is therefore indirect: Economic modernization raises living and educational standards and liberates people from a certain kind of fear brought on by life close to the subsistence level."[4] So, Fukuyama would argue, the minute a nation is free from its concentration on subsistence, it automatically desires Western liberal democracy. The assumption is that if everyone had a London, New York, or Paris middle-class standard of living, they would set aside their indigenous cultures of centuries in favor of Western liberal democracy.

Deputy Secretary Talbott reflects this assessment when, in defining America's national interest in promoting democracies, he says:

It's an issue not just of moralpolitik, but of realpolitik. Why? Because democracies are more likely to be reliable partners in trade and diplomacy and more likely to pursue foreign and defense policies that are compatible with American interests. Democracies are less likely to go to war with each other, to unleash tidal waves of refugees, to create environmental catastrophes, or to engage in terrorism. . . . The larger and more closely knit the community of democracies, the safer and more prosperous we Americans will be.[5]

The appropriateness of democracy as a form of government is not at issue here. The symbol of democracy and all its related terms are not being sold as facts; they are fetishes, pure and simple. In perceptual space, democracy has traveled far from the semantic referent of a certain way of taking care of political decision making. First, it is fetishized into a process with inherently advantageous results on its own, quite apart from situational externalities and contingencies or from any historically used referent of the term. Second, separated from its cultural underpinnings, it is a political process gratuitously given the honor of being the only "human" way of governing.

There is no conspiracy here, no lofty ideals, no complex rationale. It is a pragmatic matter of the response of foreign policy to the political economy of building "the bridge to the twenty-first century." As Western nations confront unprecedented levels of international market competition, they simply have to find a more efficient, less costly way to maintain their traditional competitive edge. In the marketplace of symbols and ideas, the ideology of democracy has an established market presence, is affordable, and the discourse about democracy is already a recognizable currency within the global market parlance. Once established as a "global brand," democracy would transcend the particularities of individual nations and their culture-based interpretative frames of evaluation and judgment. President Clinton, speaking to the French National Assembly:

There is a language of democracy spoken among nations. It is expressed in the way we work out our differences, in the way we treat each other's citizens, and in the way we honor each other's heritage. It is the language our two republics have spoken with each other for over 200 years. It is the language that the Western Allies spoke during the Second World War.

Now we have the opportunity to hear the language of democracy spoken across this entire continent.[6]

American and European comparative power is overwhelmingly massive. However, once one gets beyond such comparisons, Western developed nations are still faced with meeting a domestic constituency bottom line that far exceeds either resources available at Cold War advantage or traditional market competitive edge. Various foreign policy elites in the West agree that the cost of Cold War strategies can no longer be borne. With particular reference to America, former Secretary of State Henry Kissinger stated: "President Clinton and his foreign-policy advisers have come to power in an America that can no longer afford all the obligations of the cold-war period. They face a situation in which diplomacy and economics must replace the militarization of the two-power world."[7] Reflecting the Clinton administration's pragmatic acknowledgment of this domestic reality, Warren Christopher said, "The Iron Curtain must not be replaced with a veil of indifference if open markets and open societies are to prevail across a continent at peace."[8]

Developing countries see their own difficulties as real and immediate, unrelated to the seemingly peripheral principles and symbols concocted by Western intellectual elites. They want aid and want it now from an America and Europe unable to deliver as in the past. At the 1972 United Nations' environmental conference in Stockholm and again at the Rio conference in 1992, many developing nations were willing to sign whatever documents liberal democracies presented if the aid program in those documents were actually delivered. Then, when nothing materially happened, the developing world commitment to their dictums and principles evaporated into thin air.

FOUND: A FRIEND AND AN ENEMY

Democracy is the friend, or in President Clinton's words, "the glue that can cement economic reforms and security cooperation."[9] But where is the "superglue" that only a credible enemy can provide? Contrary to common understanding, the establishment of a new enemy may not be as difficult as one might think. This is especially so if the enemy can be so constructed that democracy and free markets are the only way it can be handled or controlled. It is a clearly pragmatic question. If the "market democracies" campaign did not fit the assumptions of European elites and American and European constituencies, it would not be used.

Fundamentally, there are three response options. The first would be to explore replacing the former Soviet Union with China. This strategy has been used and tested with lackluster results and even less support from decision makers throughout the West. Despite the pressure of human rights activists, the "market" side of "market democracy" is definitely transcendent. In any case, China only barely fills the enemy profile and its market is sorely needed in both the long and short term.

Second, they could replace the former Soviet Union with Muslim countries. After nearly fifty years of being character assassinated as the "religion of terrorists," Western intellectuals are now debating whether Islam or Confucianism would be possible candidates for the new "evil force" in Western foreign policy. The media have weighed in to the debate with their own labeling. For example, of all the atomic bombs that exist in Christian, Hindu, and Jewish nations, the only one to receive a religious appellation, the "Islamic bomb," is Pakistan's. How quickly we forget that the only atomic bomb detonated on a human population was a "Christian bomb." Nevertheless, given the market and resource implications, the effects of making over one billion Muslims the "enemy" certainly would be as harmful to the Western economies as it might only be slightly advantageous to their foreign policy.

The third, and the most likely alternative—perhaps in partial combination with any of the above—is the physical and economic risk and uncertainty Western nations believe will be created by non-democratic forces or any force that threatens free markets. For the Clinton administration, and for those G8 nations joining in the discourse, this is the new enemy of choice. As President Clinton's first Natural Security Advisor, Anthony Lake, said, "The post–Cold War era is, as we see every day, a very dangerous time. . . . [C]onflicts in this era take place more within nations than among them."[10] President Clinton believes democracy will curtail risk because "we know democracies are less likely to wage war, to violate human rights, to break treaties."[11]

The assumption here is that, without an extraordinary exertion of power to save the world from anarchy, the world's normally institutionalized safety precautions are simply not enough to allow day-to-day peace of mind. Supposedly, the threat to "order" is unprecedented and exceptional; it demands an unprecedented and exceptional response. There will be a drive to identify the actions of a small group of Western nations as being those actions needed by all countries threatened by physical risk. There will be an even stronger effort to create the presumption that America and developed European nations should be

asked to protect the "global community" from the risk of losing universalized Western values by the actions of non-democratic, non-free market states and "rogue" nations.

This approach to protection from risk satisfies all the criteria for a
new enemy and fits the kind and scale of power developed Western nations have at hand. First, in the short term, it implies the exchange of capacities and resources (military power and institutional coalescence and
validation) already in inventory. As Lake put it in classic Cold War
terms, America will be involved in "countering the 'aggression' and
supporting the 'liberalization' of 'states hostile to democracy and markets.'"[12] Second, the ideological themes clustered around unfettered
"democracy" and "free markets," with the assumptions of the hidden
hand of free political participation and free economic competition,
clearly support the image of the West as protector. But, more importantly, the physical and political risk justifies the need for setting aside
bothersome ideas about the primacy of sovereignty in favor of the bureaucratization of international morality.

And finally, because the threat of turbulence will be so ambiguous
and so universalized, "risk" situations can be highlighted or disre-
garded in terms of Western developed nations' temporary interests and
changing postures. This last point is a critical part of the inherent advantages of the policy. In this newer approach, when and to whom
Western nations respond is left to their own discretion and their own
timing. Turbulent events in this current history, filled with risky opportunities for timely intrusion, seem to offer an almost endless number of
agenda-sensitive choices.

Disarmingly simple in its presentation, Western elites and their employers assume that all nations agree, or will eventually agree, that free
markets and democracy—by virtue of the processes themselves—can
rectify the problems of all nations. The power of the "hidden hand" of
democracy and free markets is seen more in its negation than in its affirmation: Political or economic failure is made the "fault" of those who
either reject or are just very bad at using the natural human processes of
democracy and free markets. This leads to the conclusion that democracy could handle most problems if it were not for such enemies or inept managers.

This is, unfortunately, the first use of power of a third kind: Place
power outside human choice, separate politics from culture, and place
them in ambiguous, intellectually shaped constructs. Then, using these
discretionary definitions and constructs, the West can pass judgment

under assumptions that allow the "judge" to operate within a position of hegemonic exceptionality.

This is not an entirely cynical process. Developed Western nations see it as proper that they determine the success or failure of any nation's attempt to operate as a democracy or as a free market. Even while they admit exaggeration of the terms, Western intellectuals still believe that the process is fundamentally natural and human. This belief in the projected terms is in no way diminished, even when Western intellectuals recognize the power to be gained by manipulating them. To these intellectuals, the terms are so "natural" that they mark the end of history and the end of a need to discuss any alternative approaches to the liberal democratic political process.

When the West creates a fetish of democracy and free markets, they pose a danger to the actual realization of democracy in the developing world. Choosing to be a market democracy is no longer a simple matter of selecting the best government and economic structure. Acceptance by a nation presumes that they agree that democracy, human rights, and free markets are inherently human, inherently neutral, globally universal, and devoid of any cultural or political origins.

This is an eerily familiar choice, but with a particularly dangerous post–Cold War risk. There are new friends and new enemies with a similar dividing line set down by the West. It is no longer communism vs. democracy, but a forced choice of yes or no to democracy and free markets as defined by the West. This attempt to control the definition is the essential difference between Cold War strategies and post–Cold War strategies. If developing nations are willing to accept a Western form of democracy and are willing to operate as a free market regardless of the domestic economic consequences, they are no longer contenders for "rogue" nation status. They are no longer a risk to the "global community" and can be assumed to be less likely to break the global peace, do harm to their own citizens, or disrupt the smooth operation of the global economy. So then, when non-Western nations are unwilling to give their constituencies the "natural human political and economic rights" due them, this global "hidden hand" supposition works to set them apart from the world community as a potential threat.

The benefits to Western nations are those that would accrue to any nation capable of wielding such definitional power. However, the achievement of these benefits is not a forgone conclusion. This is now a more complicated non-insular world, affording as much transparency for developed nations as for developing ones. Thus the long-term strategy for economic and political dominance must offer the highest possible flexibility.

High mobility of military power, so much a part of the superpowers' planning in the 1970s and 1980s, must now be joined with an equally mobile and moment-to-moment process of defining global and domestic political and institutional positions. Except for treaties required for economic restructuring, important strategic interests, or short-term institutional and alliance relationships, future commitments must be restricted to more limited exchanges. In this new scenario, all strategies will be given second place to anything that might restrict this "in and out" flexibility. Achieving such an optimal condition will have to take greatest possible advantage of the American and European edge in the global electronic communications industry. Like media programming itself, the entire process must be episodic with as much range for impromptu framing and "in and out" involvement as possible.

In the short term, most developed Western nations will be moving in and out of the capabilities and resources of the Cold War warehouse and in and out of developing countries. They will be buying time while they restructure their economies and their international policies. This restructuring needs to happen as far away as they can get from dependent or even interdependent relationships with non-strategic developing countries.

Before discussing the current American foreign policy strategy as found in their public discourse, two points must be established. First, if developing country intellectuals are going to recognize the very real threat such transnational intrusion represents to the integrity of developing nations, they must first get beyond the mystification built into utopian images of a "global village." They must have a clear understanding of the objectives of "globalism" in the proposed "universal global culture." Second, they must go beyond the usual understanding of the term "ethnocentrism."

A BRIEF VISIT TO THE "GLOBAL VILLAGE"

Globalization has many definitions, but the most prominent among them is "the crystallization of the entire world as a single place."[13] This is a perceptual definition, which, like the referent of "nation," is not referring so much to borders as it is to a conceptual entity.[14] Without any excursion into esoteric discussions about the two-sided nature of language, it is important to understand what "global" has come to mean in the twentieth century. In language, most descriptive terms have their already recognized opposite where the application of one implies the other; good implies bad, dark implies light, and so forth. Politically, terms gain their power when you negatively value one term, thereby automatically granting a positive value to its opposite.

The term "global" is just beginning its trajectory from a geographical designation to a political one. "Global," "globalization," and "globalism" currently are labels in the early stages of creating their opposites. Already the magic of intellectual shaping is being pushed into the term. Consider the technological euphoria of intellectuals and policy makers in the West. Evidencing a simplistic logic sharply contrasting with the complexity of their high-tech tools, the new wave intellectuals conclude that, because everyone will be in global communication, the world will necessarily be in more universal agreement over issues of morals, politics, religion, and so forth. Such optimism flies in the face of experience, where increased global proximity has had the opposite effect. As one extensive analysis found, "globalization in the domains of communication and information, far from creating a sense of common human purpose, interest and value, has arguably served to reinforce the significance of identity and difference, further stimulating the 'nationalization' of politics."[15]

Numerous studies support this assessment of the impact of global communication. An early 1970s study of mass media in multicultural Yugoslavia found that "it is entirely too optimistic to believe that the media have the power to cause either social mobilization or attitude change. . . . [T]hey are effective only if there are no other interfering variables." In the case of Yugoslavia, interference with the universalization of values came from ethnic marginality and ethnically specific media content: "[B]oth of these, if unchecked, tend to reinforce the competitiveness between groups."[16] Now, over twenty years later, the memory of bloody Bosnian conflicts gives pause to the assumption that global communication can automatically create "one world." In the early 1990s, Turkey's media was radically changed with the advent of private and commercial television and radio stations. As the coverage available to Turkish citizens expanded, so did access to information about their own culture. As one study found, "[T]he new [global] media were instrumental in bringing to the fore the defining tensions of the Turkish identity, such as ethnic origin, religion, language, and group aspirations."[17]

Again, developing nation intellectuals cannot allow the absence or distortion of truth in such widely touted themes to cloud their understanding of the difference between fact and fetishized symbols. It is not in the reality of the factual referent but in the political utility of the symbol that power is found. Whether true in its thematic statement or not, the capacity of a symbol for creating a manipulable opposite is a resource of power available to those ready and able to use power of a third kind. Too often, developing nation elites think an argument is won as soon as a theme has been proven wrong. In electronically contrived non-insular space, the very act of confronting a term gives the energy of exposure to the powerful space between a term and its opposite. This is a space filled with the power of recognizable narrative. Despite the veracity of a factual referent, the repetition and resonation of paired opposites gives life to the process of mobilizing meaning for control. Thus arguments held at the level of "yes-it-is, no-it-isn't" actually empower a false theme, rather than undermining it—even when its falsity is demonstrated.

This entire effort alters the term "global," shifting its meaning away from a spatial concept embracing a complexity of human created nations, cultures, and ethnic groups. When one promotes the concept that there are universal human values that transcend culture, "global" becomes an abstract term whose only referent is an abstract moral position. This renders the term, its frameworks, and narratives available for the West to characterize cultures, nations, and ethnic groups as actively blocking the hope that people might "get together" in a global village.

Once a term is pushed by the power of a movement like technological optimism, it takes on an energy of its own, an energy capable of elevating once marginal terms to platforms of political importance. Globalists' technological optimism becomes an operative part of an intensely interactive arena of political and ideological competition. In this arena, symbols like "global" and "universal" carry narratives that become the powerful subtext of scripts filled with definite political agendas and easily described heroes and villains.

Therefore, when "universality" is seen as a realizable and positive goal and the fact of a more global world is tied to the "need to be more global," universality moves from an objective to a value. As a value, it easily becomes a criteria for evaluating the "goodness" or "badness" of human action, and a very effective political tool, indeed. Individuals and nations can find themselves locked into defined roles as out-of-date traditionalists or as marginalized entities unable to cope with life in the global village. Given enough repetition and resonation, terms with specific agendas expand to connote specific narratives. In the world of global communication, this is how democracy, human rights, and free markets can, as symbols, be elevated to universal human values.

This is all a part of the alchemy of power of a third kind. Before the effort to transform the meaning of "global," the term "ethnocentric" indicated an inescapable fixation on one's own assumptions as being right. It assumed that cultures would tend to be different and that such a condition was a hindrance to people working and thinking together. Then, the opposite of ethnocentric was "worldly." Now, the opposite of ethnocentric is "global." In this symbolic turn of the wrist, ethnocentrism becomes a label in the hands of the "universal" global political values of the West. Rather than pointing to the inherent differences of nations, "ethnocentric" now indicates those nations that are non-global, non-Western, and not democratic enough to be members of "peace-loving nations."

This is the remarkable nature of symbols whose referents are other symbols ready to cue narratives and attach responsibility. Take the "market democracy" campaign. The "globalists" give fertile ground to the promotion of universal democracy and free markets. If democracy and free markets are a solution to conflict and turbulence, then its opposite—not enough democracy and not enough free trade—could legitimize interference to bring any global disruption to an end. And because the technology over which globalists are so optimistic is controlled by a few Western nations, this places the means of defining shared morals, politics, religion, and other aspects of culture in the hands of those nations with enough power to create and project the definitions.

LIBERAL DEMOCRACY AS AN IDEOLOGICAL RESOURCE

For the past two centuries, Western intellectuals have argued that the East and the South are either inscrutable or hard-headed traditionalists. To save these nations from themselves, Western elites have always felt that they should manipulate, discount, or militarily suppress those countries that got in the way of their economic or political intentions. Now that the evil empire narrative can only be found on the discount books table, it is a matter of communicating yet another "inherent human truth" to all developing nations seen stumbling outside the path of

Western creedal righteousness. Riding the technological optimism of the intellectual elite into a global world, Western leaders can draw upon their traditional source of policy justification to create a rhetoric of democracy and free markets.

Facing a rapidly maturing ideological system, the world can see that the West is actively engaged in attempting to impose a universal way of interpreting globally communicated events. This is the "mobilization of discourse," a way of "mobilizing meaning" and narrowing available options for giving meaning to situations.[18] Thus intellectuals and politicians in the West are armed with a once unimagined technical ability to reach most people in the world. They also are fully knowledgeable and trained in human susceptibility to attractive, well-planned communication. Without the experience of the Cold War, this gathering of material and technical resources would be awesome. But Western foreign policy intellectuals have fifty years of trial and error in the global projection of ideology. When this is added to the prodigious wealth of resources and de facto control of international institutions, an unprecedented potential for deferential political control begins to emerge.

This global campaign is meant to establish a particular ethnocentrism as "natural" to all human beings and societies. The intrinsic power of the symbol package used in this campaign must be equal to the global reach of the communications system. This is an ideological campaign in its most crude form: human beings wanting other human beings to give meaning to events in ways that serve the best interests of the nation doing the mobilizing. Being effective in altering the frames of others in ways positive to one's specific objectives has certain minimum prerequisites. First, it is necessary to make certain that the frames are part of the actual events and situations being experienced and not allowed to remain in the abstract. Then, such efforts must enter the stream of the target population's everyday life. Finally, their creation must begin with entirely known concepts or themes because to do otherwise is too costly and time consuming.

It is understood that meeting this challenge lies in the advantage and the disadvantage of global access itself. This global access is two-way and, as such, it presents a disadvantage of unprecedented transparency to anyone trying to turn that access to advantage. The campaign effort is an observable and an entirely concrete event open at every moment to critical perception and comment—when that perception is tutored. The rhetoric of neutrality must be reflected in the appearance of neutrality in the campaign itself.

The democracy themes and the identity of the West as the cradle of democracy have the advantage of a long-term history and a recent half-century of investment. "Democracy" is already shelved and ready for use in the institutionalized repository of often repeated Western intellectual constructs. Nowhere are they more readily recognized and affirmed than in America and Europe. In the case of American foreign policy, the past half century has been characterized by the American assumption that it must take on the burden of "making the world safe for democracy" because "if America doesn't do it, who will?" In effect, Western nations have been thoroughly educated in this belief of an historically derived mission as well as the assumption that along with this mission goes a good deal of the right to exceptional treatment. Throughout this century, the West has not spared developing nations and their peoples from this fundamental assumption. Thus "democracy" as a rationale for exceptionality is hardly a new idea. It is in inventory and, once refurbished for a non–bi-polar and non-insular world, it may be just as fresh and viable as it was for planners after World War II.

When the ideologist has access to the awareness of people, he can demonstrate a relationship between the meaning normally given to a situation and the "new" frame. These efforts have an organic quality. They create associations and positive connections between democracy and its protector, or democracy and the "right to choose," or democracy and "freedom of choice." Once the connection is made, other meanings and associated desirable scenarios can be added through the manipulation of events. In this way, Western nations' actions can be presented through globally familiar narratives.

Fortunately for Western nations, comprehending and making sense of events happens in the fast traffic of human subjectivity. It is in subjective thought where congruity and incongruity, clear coherence and confused muddling, pass happily with remarkably few accidents. There is no need to try to change attitudes about definitions or identities with nations or broad cultural themes. "Democracy" and "freedom of choice" as global brands become favorable ways of ascribing either positive or negative meaning to targeted events.

Again, this is not a one-to-one process. One does not have to produce an entirely "democratic" event to sell democracy or an entirely "Western" event to sell the West. The entire interpretative process is more partial, subject to alteration and respondent to all sorts of events than is a simple one-to-one scenario. We are not talking on the level of dictionary definitions here. Dictionary definitions are just research reports about the way people have been found to use words. "Democracy" may be defined in a certain way in the dictionary, but that definition is not what "democracy" should be or how it is actually perceived by a certain set of people at a certain time. Nor is it the way professional ideologists see "democracy."

A positive global identity becomes associated with the well-being of the individual confronting events connected to that specific identity. In fact, in this campaign, there is no need for a "real" intention to create "free markets" and "democracies" in a global sense. It is not a priority that every country actually become a democracy. The real priority is to get elites and their middle-class constituencies to want, for themselves, the positive experience associated with democracy. Once that objective has been met, opportunities can be created for the discretionary enforcement of free markets in instances compatible with a Western nations' agenda. This assumes, of course, that such a consensus will create pressure to accept the use of that term for judging the actions of other nations and peoples.

This is especially true in the world of power of a third kind. Here, the speed of the media reflects the speed of thought presented within continuous sight and sound of one event after another, interrupted only by commercials and sudden moves to another channel. With this kind of timing, how many are running to the dictionary to get the definition of "democracy" or "human rights?" The term "McDonalds," has little to do with the actual comparative taste of the hamburgers served; it is, rather, the *experience* of McDonalds that is sold. At one point, a toy gift being given away with the hamburgers was so popular that customers came in for the toy, leaving the hamburgers behind. When McDonalds tried to open in India, a non–meat-eating culture, they faced opposition. Once the meat was changed, the restaurant opened to eager crowds. Because McDonalds is a "global brand," it has transcended the referent hamburger and moved the participant to an experience that has melded with the term.

The mobilization of ideology as culturally transcendent symbols in the "in and out" foreign policy campaign requires a careful economy in demands made of the target population. The terms are inflated into universal and global shape, while the strategies and tactics are tightly focused and utterly discretionary. In effect, the objective of the campaign is to create a form of participation that appears to have little concrete consequence when, in fact, the consequence is a significant loss of actual individual and national choice. This is a prime criteria in the political economy of power of a third kind: Keep the actual commitment of the sender and the perceived commitment of the receiver at the lowest possible levels of material, psychological, and political expenditure.

Events will occur or will be caused to occur. With the "global brand" of democracy carried forward in front of the camera from reporter to anchorman and repeated by statesmen and non-governmental organizations (NGOs), the question for strategists is not a question of who, what, or even where. For Western nations capable of using power of a third kind, the important questions are the "when" of timing and the "how" of interposing Western frames and narratives in the context of events with a clear cost-free/risk-free, carefully planned exit. Marshall McLuhan may have been right when he claimed that the medium was the message. In power of a third kind foreign policy, the events and the media are the medium. The message is created by the strategic intrusion of the politician into the mainstream of the televised narrative.

The marvelous compressing of distance, granted by the electronic wonder of television, virtually eliminates the need for a physical presence. Finite constraints of physical space are largely replaced by the nearly limitless plasticity of mental space. Far from being the intractable hindrance created by Western anthropologists, culture is the all too ready workshop of the intellectual as ideologist. Here he constructs his transcendent frameworks from the rich production created by the cumulative acts of indigenous cultures. Once the interpretative boundaries of culture are known, frame-event associations can be established without the risk of creating conflict with local culture.

The access afforded by the reach of electronic media into the mental space of nearly all developing peoples allows the ideologist the formidable possibilities of the power of cultural transcendence. This new capacity is so much more real, more powerful, more efficient, and so much less costly than traditional instruments of power. No matter how impressive, a gunboat in the harbor is both too risky and too costly—especially in a world so interdependent and so conflictual that there are just too many harbors to cover.

FIRST USES OF POWER OF A THIRD KIND

America is the clear leader in articulating a foreign policy based on the emergence of power of a third kind. Other Western members of the G8 are either following America's lead or just letting America extend itself. This will change as the policy strategy gains strength and the full implications of this power are more clearly realized. Beneath the arguments of the G8 meetings over telecommunications issues are questions of just who, how, and in what circumstances global communications will be accessed and used. This is an era of consensus creation among developed Western nations regarding proper roles and actions. The confrontation between these major players should not cloud the fact that these roles and actions are being contested and confirmed with the clear intention of finding a compatible site for cooperation. Nor should anyone miss the fact that cooperation will be found within entirely Western cultural and political assumptions.

Events affected by global transparency and non-insularity are moving at such a rapid pace that, had this book been written in the early 1990s, there would not have been a clear example of just how power of a third kind might be understood to work. In effect, it would have been an entirely theoretical, if not futuristic work. The first and most extensive use of this power was initiated by the Clinton administration. Like all other realizations of the immanent power of technology, its actual uses fall far short of its potential. At some point, however, technique overcomes technology and yet another form of power emerges.

When the Clinton administration entered office in 1993, it stepped onto the world stage at a time when the United States' role as single superpower remained undefined. This administration was predisposed to placing foreign policy second in priority after domestic interests or, at best, to focus only on those foreign-policy interests that promoted domestic issues. This lack of definition created a vacuum between government and the traditional foreign-policy elites. The response among pundits and foreign-policy intellectuals to this vacuum was not positive. Characterizing the policies of the new government as anything from "inadequate" to "incompetent" became an almost everyday editorial and commentary item. During his tenure as National Security Advisor in the first Clinton administration, Anthony Lake was given the job of providing an intellectual defense of their foreign policy:

Some people, in a curious bit of nostalgia for the Cold War, complain that our policy lacks a single, over-arching principle—that it can't be summed up on a bumper sticker. But while we are operating in a radically new international environment, America's fundamental mission endures. *The same ideas that were under attack by communism and before that by fascism remain under attack today, as we are seeing in the Middle East.* Now, as then, we are defending an idea that has many names—tolerance, liberty, civility, pluralism, but that shows a constant face—the face of the democratic society.[19]

It would be nine months into the first term before the Clinton foreign-policy team presented anything like a foreign-policy rationale and it would be well into their first year in office before administration officials began a direct aggressive campaign to lay out the government's foreign-policy approach. The call among the foreign-policy establishment was for a vision and a plan of action to assure that America would enter the twenty-first century firmly placed to enjoy the "American Century." Few of them felt Clinton's staff and advisors had the capacity for such planning, and even fewer believed that Clinton had the interest or the drive to carry out an admittedly difficult agenda in the post–Cold War world.

Eventually, the Clinton people did present a foreign-policy approach they called the American "Strategy of Enlargement." Expanding American markets around the world was linked to democracy as the victor of the Cold War. American economic interests—the subtext of the "Containment Policy" of the Cold War—had been moved to center stage. The Clinton administration saw that the world was safe for democracy; their goal now was for democracy to make the world safe for free and open trade.

Clinton's pragmatic foreign policy would use themes reflecting American values. Assuming that "democracy and human rights are inseparable," they therefore "need to . . . help democracy and market economics take root in those regions of greatest humanitarian concern."[20] The Clinton administration believed that these values would resonate among the American people to gain their support. The administration also believed that their pragmatism would appeal to a conservative American Congress and multinational elites.

Malleable policy objectives are reflected in the process approach adopted by the administration. In 1985, nearly a decade before becoming President Clinton's National Security Advisor, Lake assessed the implications of future United States policy toward radical regimes in this way: "Policies can best be shaped, therefore, by asking questions about each situation rather than by pretending to know the theoretical answers even before the questions are posed."[21] This inductive approach clearly reflects a White House consensus on the need for adaptability. Cries from critics for concrete objectives fell on deaf ears as the

Clinton administration policy followed the flexible approach of "guidelines" instead of "precepts." President Clinton characterized his policy approach by saying, "We have to drop the abstractions and dogma and pursue, based on trial and error and persistent experimentation, a policy that advances our values of freedom and democracy, peace and security."[22]

Speaking at the School of Advanced International Studies at Johns Hopkins University in September 1993, Lake couched the foreign policy of the United States in just these terms: "Billions of people on every continent are simply concluding, based on decades of their own hard experience, that democracy and markets are the most productive and liberating ways to organize their lives."[23] After this initial connection between democracy and markets, Lake became more explicit: "During the Cold War, even children understood America's security mission. As they looked at those maps on their schoolroom walls, they knew we were trying to contain the creeping expansion of that big, red blob. Today, at great risk of oversimplification, we might visualize our security mission as promoting the enlargement of the 'blue areas' of market democracies."[24]

In fact, in this speech, Lake "used the word 'market' no less than forty-one times."[25] This is the true difference: Market democracy has replaced the drive to make "a world safe for democracy," the theme so recognizable in Cold War ideological combat. At Johns Hopkins, Lake was quite unabashed in presenting the administration's priorities:

> Beyond seeing to our base, the second imperative for our strategy must be to help democracy and markets expand and survive in other places where we have the strongest security concerns and where we can make the greatest difference. This is not a democratic crusade; it is a pragmatic commitment to see freedom take hold where that will help us most. . . . We must focus our efforts where we have the most leverage.[26]

America's Western values were touted as universal values, and the Clinton administration defined market dominance as the nation's number one security interest. Protecting the planet and the universal rights of the individual would facilitate any need to supersede the sovereign rights of a nation. This is a pragmatic strategy that requires international acceptance of Western exceptionality, Western definitions of universal values, and a willingness to let America lead other Western nations as global protector and promoter of those values.

Lake emphasized that market democracies "protect our interests and our security, at the same time reflecting values which are American and universal."[27] This is ethnocentrism on a new global scale, in all its unembarrassed presumption. While the assumption that American values are the natural values for all men is explicit in the term "universal," it is important to note what is *not* in this statement: The projection of such "universal" values is not presented here because they are needed by the world, nor are they presented in terms of some opposite non-human or evil force. Rather, the purpose is simply pragmatic. If democracy will help us get markets, fine. If no democracy is possible, fine. The test of the policy is not the existence or non-existence of democracy; the test of foreign policy is, by this statement, whatever "pragmatic commitment will help us the most."

Subsequently, Lake is more specific as to which countries will receive the focus of this pragmatic effort: "those with large economies, critical locations, nuclear weapons or the potential to generate refugee flows into our own nation or into key friends and allies."[28] Thus while there is an assumption of the universal need for democracy and Western values, there is absolutely no need to get in a crusade to establish those values. The effort will be targeted to specific countries and locations. There is, however, the assumption that where such access is needed for markets, the establishment of some form of democracy is better for attaining that access.

The bridge for the transition between the Cold War and post–Cold War had finally been designed. Just three months after his Johns Hopkins speech, Lake, in a speech to the Council on Foreign Relations in New York, made explicit that the "market" took precedence over "democracy" in American foreign policy: "And the benefits to America are clear. When old command economies turn to the market, they generate a huge appetite for American exports. Furthermore, free markets create middle classes. Middle classes favor the emergence of democratic governments that accommodate ethnic diversity, protect the rights of their citizens and enhance stability."[29]

Creating "a huge appetite for American exports" comprehends the essential elements of the Clinton foreign policy. Markets dovetail beautifully with democracy and, the administration believes, the "hidden hand" within the process of democracy and free markets will ultimately be salutary to the economic, political, and social growth of all countries and peoples.

Politically, the facile assumption is that, if the decisions of all peoples are taken into account in some form of representative government, democracy will be effective, despite the complexities of culture and history. What the Clinton administration would like to assume is that all this freedom to consume and vote will create a "huge appetite" in the global village. Free markets create happily spending people who will "favor the emergence of democratic governments."

The linkage between this policy and its rationale of reaching the democratized middle classes is exactly the point where the economic objectives and the ideological objectives of Western governments converge. Again, words do not just refer to events. Rather, as constructed fetishes, they form the frames and the vehicles for power. Former Secretary of State Warren Christopher, in a statement confirming America's view of its centrality in the world, said: "We have decisively shaped the most open global trading system in history and *put America at its hub.*"[30]

Although more transparent, "market democracy" is the same pragmatic approach the West took in projecting "democratic capitalism" in its conflict with international communism from the beginning of the Cold War. However, "'democracy—yes or no' is often . . . an attempt to conceal a friend-foe setup behind the veil of an unassailable concept."[31] It is an approach with the same disparity between the romantic inflation of terms and the way they are actually experienced by developing nation consumer-citizens. However, there are two important differences. First, because democracy is seen as better for getting market access, but not as a necessary part of attaining economic security, it is less important than markets that are the primary concern. Second, the decisions being sought are not those of non-Western people as voters, but as consumers first and as voters later, if at all. In this sense, then, nations and states are placed second to individuals. A "healthy appetite" for American consumer products and consumer-citizen concepts becomes both the object and the channel for the establishment of America as the source satisfying the needs of citizens and consumers as individuals.

These few Western nations will work between a developing country's nightmare of economic and political demise as dictated by political and physical safety, and the global dream of a middle-class life. All these efforts will be directed toward the individual as consumer and citizen.

The terms used go beyond coercion, force, and even classic forms of simple manipulation to the creation of transcultural frameworks. Consider the rhetoric and the intention in President Clinton's statement to CNN journalists during a global interview: "Now the greatest opportunity for our security is to help enlarge the world's communities of market democracies and to move toward a world in which all the great powers govern by a democratic plan. If we do, we'll have more valuable partners in trade, and better partners in diplomacy and security."[32] Anthony Lake stated the same premise in his Johns Hopkins speech but in more explicit and pragmatic terms: "Unless the major market democracies can act together . . . the fierce competition of the new global economy, coupled with the end of our common purpose from the Cold War, could drive us into prolonged stagnation or even economic disaster."[33]

If this campaign is successful, America and its G8 colleagues' nightmare of an evolving order they cannot control and a material vision they might not be able to afford can be set aside. Instead, they can dream of quiescent, happily consuming nations following in the footsteps of Western history. Today, developing countries feel as pushed as the Western nations by the threat of anarchy and the loss of even low levels of affluence. The Western nations' hope is that foreign elites and middle classes will join the Western constituencies in being susceptible to the moment-to-moment electronic framing of events in Western terms and within the parameters of Western agenda.

This analysis of the campaign could illicit the criticism that it overestimates the power of Western ideologists and strategic planners. Admittedly, there is no clear evidence that Western ideologists have any real understanding of the viewer and power of a third kind on this more sophisticated level. However, it is best to remember that the full implications of a particular technological change have always been fully explored by its creators and others.

In this transition and well into the next century, power of a third kind will be used by the developed Western nations to manipulate the subjective perception of events and the globally perceived intentions behind Western actions in relation to these events. At this time, the Clinton administration will intrude into events associated with democracy and free markets in order to frame those events in positive and predictable ways. They can do this with full confidence in the world-wide reach of the privatized corporate media system, advertisers, and narrative-structured reporters—all against the backdrop of discourse managed and coordinated by America and its G8 partners. In the end, a successful effort would limit both the alternative possible frameworks and the actual alternative choices.

THE MECHANICS OF UNIVERSAL ETHNOCENTRISM

In this post-insular "age of Internet," Western action in developing countries will respond to four basic guidelines. First, military and economic power will be used as primary measures only in the case of vital strategic interests and almost never without the concerted involvement of other Western and regional non-Western nations. Second, Western nations will only participate in a conflict when the victory is certain and when favorable themes can be amplified as a part of the conflict. Third, such involvement will only be attractive when a small group of Western nations and America, in particular, can be seen as clear leaders of the coalesced effort. Fourth, except in those cases of urgent strategic interest, the risk of engagement will be evaluated relative to the potential for gaining exceptional low-risk access to resources and markets.

These guidelines will result in a strategy that will not only *use* the electronic media, it will *reflect* its process and structure. In a spaceless world, the event will be important *despite* rather than *because* of the place it occurs. The event will first be evaluated in terms of the universality of Western frameworks and how it projects their image as global protector and judge. Second, it will be evaluated in terms of the degree of interest it holds for targeted domestic and international publics. Third, it will be evaluated according to the ability of the event to meet a rigid standard of cost-conscious efficiency and lowest possible political risk.

In 1996, when Taiwan held its first democratic elections, all the narrative elements were evident for a clear demonstration of power of a third kind. China, the non-democratic nation of Tiananmen Square, was holding naval maneuvers and seeming to threaten the free market democracy of Taiwan during its elections. Also, the media was already in Taiwan to report the election, so the event would receive world-wide coverage. The least expensive and most risk-free exposure of Western themes was at hand. Send a carrier to the site and have the United States naval commander say, "China has a good navy, but the American navy is the strongest in the world." So, not only was light shone upon a foe to democracy but, more importantly, the United States was pictured as ready and willing to protect those that stand for the right to choose their own government.

When Liberia moved into a state of chaos and insurgency, the situation offered absolutely no opportunity to reinforce Western themes and, therefore, Western nations' actions were correspondingly low key to nonexistent. Despite the fact that Liberia was used as a model of democracy in Africa, that it was a launching area for American interests in Western Africa, and had its beginnings in America even to the point of mimicking the American flag, the United States stayed only long enough to get its citizens out and protect its embassy. Liberia did not meet the resource-market criteria and, given its Somalia-like anarchical ambiance, it failed in its ability to positively project either the identity of democracy or America on prime time news. On the contrary, it portrayed the miracle of democracy *not* working in a country whose governing processes were midwifed by the United States.

At other times the power of an event, as portrayed by the media, will create a response—especially as it touches the emotions of American constituencies. Lake's pragmatic policies did not suggest American involvement in the Bosnian conflict. In fact, some Washington analysts believed that "the administration [had] already calibrated our interests as too small to warrant decisive military action." Nevertheless, "the decision [to use air power] was made on the basis of TV pictures. What changed American policy was coverage of the massacre at the market."[34] This suggests a foreign policy with all the characteristics and resources of any sophisticated domestic political campaign. In fact, that campaign has been criticized by Henry Kissinger for its "extraordinary obsession with public relations" and for "treating foreign policy as if it were a domestic issue susceptible to consensus through trade-offs."[35]

Not long after the first foreign-policy statements by President Clinton's advisers in 1993, Daniel Yankelovich, the administration's political pollster and theorist, weighed in with his own operational guidelines. He began with a criticism: "The sad truth [is] that the foreign policy community has little or no idea about engaging the public under new post–Cold War conditions." He offers several suggested stages of action to rectify this void: raise awareness of developing problems, impart a sense of urgency, recognize and combat citizen resistance. He urges the use of "trial balloons [and] choice work."[36] It is more than just interesting that "the Kennedys reached out to Robert Frost. . . . The Reagans had Frank Sinatra. For better and for worse, Yankelovich is likely to serve as a significant intellectual standard-bearer of the Clinton years."[37]

Again, the exertion of power always shapes intention to its most important instruments. Foreign policy by ratings and canny predictions of likely responses to breaking events is, like the media itself, a necessary part of an in-and-out policy. Keeping the show going and establishing program lines carries equal weight with more concrete results.

Thus all the attacks on the Clinton administration's policy fail to recognize that it is, in fact, a post-insular policy that relies more on the process of perceiving and being perceived than on steadfast positions and unchanging postures. This foreign policy demands "the right to choose" and, like the viewer, will fight to the death for control over the remote channel changer. Given this, it is not surprising that, in the assessments following his leaving office, Warren Christopher was criticized for his lack of ability to give the media "concepts." In the world of power of a third kind foreign policy, he seemed not ready for prime time. In foreign policy today, the ability to encapsulate an act, a project, or a policy within an attractive narrative is as important as the ability to conceive or even to implement a policy.

So the resources for transition to power of a third kind are there, the commitment and the logic of that commitment is evident on the surface of current actions of the West, and of American foreign policy in particular. They will move from event to event in search of an opportunity for intrusion into the stream of events. They will select intrusions that offer the opportunity to affirm universally Western frameworks and the exceptionality they might justify. They will find and participate in events in non-strategic arenas only when they cry out for the intervention of the superpower.[38] They will emphasize situations where the only exchange required is the willingness to grant supra-national status.

This action will take full advantage of electronic communications' destruction of distance. President Clinton, when participating in a global interview with CNN reporters, said:

A global economy has collapsed distances and expanded opportunity, because of a communications revolution symbolized most clearly by CNN and what all of us are doing this evening all around the world.

We are front-row history witnesses. We see things as they occur.[39]

That critical change in global human affairs has moved intentional efforts toward control. In fact, change itself has moved from physical space to the mental space of every human being within the reach of electronic image and sound communication. We are all on the front row of history, but now the fact that we are watching is as important as the event we are watching. In the era of power of a third kind, this is true in the same way and for the same reason that the reporting of the event is more important than the event itself or the place in which it occurs.

To this point in our analysis, we have looked at change and power in this post-insular era from the standpoint of the West. Looked at from that vantage point, the process seems so self-assured, so full of resources and options, and so utterly indifferent to the responses of the non-Western world, one could be overwhelmed to the point of resignation. But there is another side. This emerging effort is desperate precisely because it is so very difficult. No matter how impressive the technology and the technical expertise underlying all this power, accomplishing a world brand framework based on Western presumptions will be much more challenging than any comparable military effort. And it will have to be maintained at a high-efficiency pitch even after intermediate goals are accomplished.

In this way, exertions of power of a third kind will be much like the Cold War. Once engaged, it will never have a clear-cut confrontation; it will always function at a high level of intense interaction, and the need to demonstrate power will be moment-to-moment, day-to-day, everyday. However, unlike the Cold War, there will be no Berlin Wall ending the continual investment in the demonstration of power. No single nation can do anything to end the striving for exceptionality. Because the enemy is non-democratic, non-free market nations, the entire program is initiated and presented as a process without a final day of victory. Because the definitions are ambiguous and idiosyncratic, it will be hard for non-Western nations to know when they are democratic or free market enough. The situation becomes an endless process of improvement validated only by a few Western nations, judging according to entirely Western criteria.

In her remarks after being sworn in as President Clinton's Secretary of State, Madeline Albright made the process starkly reminiscent of stages of growth. Now, however, there are four "stages of democracy," reflecting a nation's willingness to meet Western democracy criteria for being a member in good standing of the community of nations. Demonstrating the greatest willingness to "have" democracy are the "functioning democracies," those fully evolved countries who see their interests being served by a stable international order. Next are the "evolving democracies" who would like to move into the first category but are not yet able. "America will encourage their process," Albright said. In the third group are the "rogue" states who see an advantage to themselves in trying to disrupt the international order. Finally, there are the "failed states," which Secretary Albright promised she would work to assure do not become "wards" of the international system. The "stages of growth" have become the "stages of democracy," with a small group of Western nations having positioned themselves as judges at the top of yet another stairway. Once again they stand ready to take on the burden of "helping" developing nations toward the realization of the Western historic and cultural experience.

When the battlefield is subjectivity, the decision making and the investment are always in the present. This is a contest where the present and all future "presents" are constantly open to changes in perception, perspective, and implemented reality. Because the objective of worldwide compliance is also a point of highest vulnerability, counterpower is incipient to that process. As we shall see in Chapter Five, counterpower is a threat in proportion to the exceptionality demanded. Where the justification for that exceptionality is transparent, counterpower demands as much attention as the exertion of power itself.

This two-sided nature of electronically projected transparency is the most challenging part of the "world brand" campaign. No magician is ever applauded if the audience can see the rabbit before he pulls it out of the hat. The audience may be angry enough to demand its money back. Ironically, the reciprocal transparency of global television is necessary to facilitate demands for exceptional exclusions from reciprocal agreements. However, once the campaign effort itself is made transparent and is communicated worldwide, it becomes predictable and hardly magic. This could force a reversion to overt coercion and force and bring about a confrontation over the global consensus on sovereignty. Or one could hope that the words "free" and "multicultural" would be treated more in terms of their positive referents than in their rhetorical sound.

Western nations will find it impossible to successfully use power of a third kind if the non-Western nations' leaders simply choose a more active role than eager consumers or compliant viewers of a narrative featuring the superpower as supra-nation.

NOTES

1. William Clinton, "President Clinton's Speech at American University, February 26, 1993," *Foreign Policy Bulletin* 3 (May/June 1993): 7.

2. Strobe Talbott, "Support for Democracy and the U.S. National Interest; Deputy Secretary Talbott; Remarks Before the Carnegie Endowment for International Peace, Washington, D.C., March 1, 1996," *U.S. Department of State Dispatch* 7 (18 March 1996) [database online]: 13–14 of 29.

3. Warren Christopher, "Clinton's Foreign Policy: Internationalism, Not Isolationism," *Current* 374 (July/August 1995): 20.

4. Francis Fukuyama, "Allies or Enemies? Confucianism and Democracy," *Current* 376 (October 1995): 16.

5. Talbott, "Support for Democracy," 14.

6. William Clinton, "President Clinton's Speech to French National Assembly, Paris, June 7, 1994," *Foreign Policy Bulletin* 5 (July/August 1994): 4.

7. Henry A. Kissinger, "At Sea in a New World," *Newsweek*, 6 June 1994, p. 38

8. Christopher, "Clinton's Foreign Policy," 21.

9. Clinton, "Speech to French National Assembly," 4.

10. Anthony Lake, "Press Briefing on the 'Presidential Decision Directive,' May 5, 1994," *Foreign Policy Bulletin* 5 (July/August 1994): 72.

11. William Clinton, "President's Appearance on CNN's 'Global Forum with President Clinton,' Atlanta, May 3, 1994," *Foreign Policy Bulletin* 5 (July/August 1994): 6.

12. Daniel Williams, "Clinton's National Security Advisor Outlines U.S. 'Strategy of Enlargement,'" *Washington Post*, 22 September 1993, sec. A, p. 16, quoting Anthony Lake's speech at the School of Advanced International Studies, Johns Hopkins University, Washington, DC, 22 September 1993.

13. Roland Robertson, "Globalization and Societal Modernization: A Note on Japan and Japanese Religion," *Sociological Analysis* 47 (Summer 1987): 38, quoted in Johann P. Arnason, "Nationalism, Globalization and Modernity," in *Global Culture: Nationalism, Globalization and Modernity*, ed. Mike Featherstone. A Theory, Culture & Society Special Issue (London: SAGE Publications, 1990), 220.

14. The "global village" is used in Marshall McLuhan and Bruce R. Powers, *The Global Village: Transformations in World Life and Media in the 21st Century* (New York: Oxford University Press, 1989).

15. David Held, "Democracy and the New International Order," in *Cosmopolitan Democracy: An Agenda for a New World Order*, eds. Daniele Archibugi and David Held (Cambridge, England: Polity Press, 1995), 115.

16. Gertrude Joch Robinson, "Mass Media and Ethnic Strife in Multi-National Yugoslavia," *Journalism Quarterly* 51 (Fall 1974): 496–97.

17. Haluk Sahin and Asu Aksoy, "Global Media and Cultural Identity in Turkey," *Journal of Communication* 43 (Spring 1993): 35.

18. John B. Thompson, "Language and Ideology: A Framework for Analysis," *Sociology* 35 (1987): 516–36, referred to by Michael Billig, *Ideology and Opinions: Studies in Rhetorical Psychology*, Loughborough Studies in Communication and Discourse (London: SAGE Publications, 1991), 14.

19. Anthony Lake, "Defining Missions, Setting Deadlines: Meeting New Security Challenges in the Post–Cold War World; Address to Students and Faculty at The George Washington University, Washington, D.C., March 6, 1996," *U.S. Department of State Dispatch* 7 (18 March 1996) [database online]: 25 of 29. Italics added.

20. Anthony Lake, "The Four Pillars to Emerging 'Strategy of Enlargement,'" excerpts from a speech given at the School of Advanced International Studies, Johns Hopkins University, Baltimore, 22 September 1993, *Christian Science Monitor*, 29 September 1993, p. 19.

21. Anthony Lake, *Third World Radical Regimes: U.S. Policy Under Carter and Reagan*, Headline Series, no. 272 (New York: Foreign Policy Association, January/February 1985), 49.

22. Todd S. Purdum, "Clinton Warns of U.S. Retreat to Isolationism," *New York Times*, 7 October 1995, sec. A, p. 1, late edition.

23. Anthony Lake, "From Containment to Enlargement; Address at the School of Advanced International Studies, Johns Hopkins University, Washington, D.C., September 21, 1993," *U.S. Department of State Dispatch* 4 (September 27, 1993): 658.

24. Ibid., 659.

25. Richard Falk, "Clinton Doctrine: The Free Marketeers," *The Progressive* 58 (January 1994): 18.

26. Lake, "From Containment to Enlargement," 661.

27. "Lake Says US Interests Compel Engagement Abroad," *USIS* (23 September 1993): 8–9, quoted in Jochen Hippler, "Democratisation of the Third World After the End of the Cold War," in *The Democratisation of Disempowerment: The Problem of Democracy in the Third World*, ed. Jochen Hippler, Transnational Institute Series (London: Pluto Press, 1995), 12.

28. Ibid., 661.

29. Anthony Lake, "Effective Enlargement in a Changing World," *USIS* (20 December 1993): 21, quoted in Hippler, "Democratisation of the Third World," 14.

30. Christopher, "Clinton's Foreign Policy," 20. Italics added.

31. Jochen Hippler, "Democratisation of the Third World After the End of the Cold War," 17.

32. Clinton, "President's Appearance on CNN's 'Global Forum,'" 6.

33. Williams, "Clinton's National Security Advisor."

34. Charles Krauthammer, "Intervention Lite: Foreign Policy by CNN," *Washington Post*, 18 February 1994, sec. A, p. 25.

35. Kissinger, "At Sea in a New World," 37.

36. Daniel Yankelovich and John Immerwahr, a paper presented at the Summer 1993 American Assembly, a non-partisan public policy forum associated with Columbia University, quoted by Jim Hoagland, "Policy From the Top Down," *Washington Post*, 7 October 1993, sec. A, p. 23.

37. Hoagland, "Policy From the Top Down."

38. William I. Robinson, "Pushing Polyarchy: The U.S.–Cuba Case and the Third World," *Third World Quarterly* 16 (December 1995): 643–59.

39. Clinton, "President's Appearance on CNN's 'Global Forum,'" 5.

CHAPTER 4

Power of a Third Kind: Criteria for Success

In this post-insular, post–Cold War world, the "market democracy" campaign will be a contest between the West and the Rest. Nothing less than the way human beings will define the culture of their global village will be decided. In this period, the West will no longer be in the business of protecting nations. Saving nations was more appropriate in a bi-polar struggle. They are, however, very much in the business of promoting their new identity as protectors of the individual. Now, the struggle is over a global consensus on exceptionality. The key gambit in this contest will be symbols; among the most important of these will be "individual," "rights," and "free choice." Western nations' success with this effort requires the cumulative support of individuals in their combined role as consumers and citizens. Such exceptionality can only be gained by establishing the inherent preeminence of individual human rights over the right of national sovereignty. Grasping this perception is absolutely critical for comprehending the overall strategy. For at least the next half-century, setting aside national sovereignty in favor of the supposed need to protect human and individual rights will typify the main thrust of developing nation conflicts with developed nations.

This strategy will be tailored to the twin realities of Western strengths and weaknesses on one hand and, on the other, to the increasing sense of "risk" in a world suddenly without the rationale of the bi-polar struggle. In an atmosphere of increasing turbulence deriving from political and economic dissatisfaction, the over three thousand ethnic groups worldwide offer, on a selective basis, constant justification for intervention to protect the rights of individuals. These and other conflicts will be available to the Western nations for their discretionary use on a nearly weekly basis. This was, no doubt, Anthony Lake's meaning when he said that the United States' "strategy of enlargement" foreign policy "must counter the aggression and support the liberalization of states hostile to democracy and markets."[1]

Riding the wave of America's identification with the magically endowed words of "democracy" and "individual rights," the United States stands ready to participate in United Nations' interventions that are *not* on their list of strategic nations "when any of the following occur: a threat to or breach of international peace and security; an urgent humanitarian disaster coupled with violence; a sudden interruption of established democracy; or a gross violation of human rights coupled with violence."[2]

The ambiguity and lack of criteria aside, this is a blank check for nearly any kind of intervention. It is a remarkable statement of intent to stand above sovereignty as the judge and protector of the individual in relation to his own locally derived institutions. Given the achievement of such an intent and operating on the certainty that media coverage will narrate the action within Western values and assumptive frameworks, Western nations could nearly assume the likelihood of positive international affirmation. With this kind of resounding media and institutional legitimacy, the exercise of that exceptionality promises extremely low risk and the real potential of remarkably high gain.

This policy will be tested in developing countries and measured by the degree of exceptionality elites and middle classes are willing to grant Western nations. This is a critical point often missed by developing world intellectuals who continue to discuss ethnocentrism as though it were an anthropological or sociological question without significant political impact or content. Given the power and the commitment of the West toward universalizing these creedal assumptions, such misapprehension will result in granting the West a wide open door into other countries. Developing nations' intellectuals must update their understanding of these symbolic campaigns in general and ethnocentrism in particular. They must realize that these efforts are actually more long lasting in impact and more intrusive in their effects than any process of military or political penetration used during the Cold War.

With regard to the "market democracy" campaign, in particular, the structure of the privatized electronic communications system presents itself as a manipulable and available resource for mobilizing meaning. It is also clear that within this system, the bureaucratized intellectual plays an important role in shaping political process and separating it from culture. Two questions remain and are the focus of analysis here. What criteria must be met if this campaign is to be successful? And what is the role and importance of intergovernmental and non-governmental institutions in a campaign using power of a third kind?

CRITERIA FOR A SUCCESSFUL CAMPAIGN

What are the pivotal criteria that will decide whether this campaign of culturally loaded symbols will be successful? The generic task of mobilizing ideology has a wide and deep literature. Given the ambitious goal of establishing universal presumptions, there are some minimal requirements for success. The campaign must be able to make the liberal democratic concept of Man an inherent part of being human. It must be accepted to such an extent that actions to protect the rights assumed in Western liberalism will be considered both neutral and necessary. They must be recognizable but ambiguous enough to afford the West the discretion of interpretation, favorably associated with them even though they may be factually inaccurate. Above all, they must be internationally institutionalized as universally applicable apart from the vagaries of any specific nation or culture.

This "work" will involve the most massive mobilization of meaning in the history of human persuasion. The rhetoric of this effort will include every known technique and use every available communications technology to accomplish its aim. The use of symbols in persuasion is a time-honored tradition in the West, a field of study that reaches back in a continuous line of scholarship and practice to the time of Aristotle. Today, the Madison Avenue rhetoric of marketing products and meaning has no real competition in the rest of the world. This capacity and the techniques and talent of that entire system is readily at hand for government use. However, just any associated terms or randomly selected referents would not necessarily be adequate to meet the challenges presented by a need for universality. The chosen terms must be persuasively and dynamically connected to the single global perspective meant to be established.

The entire goal of establishing the universality of ethnocentric positions depends on achieving a degree of consensus regarding the neutrality of Western nations' transnational actions. If these Western philosophical and political concoctions can become embodied as a part of the perceived nature of Man himself, then that embodiment renders them neutral. If these rights are then accepted as universal, Western actions to protect their viability would be seen as neutral just as a doctor reviving the function of an individual's heart is seen as neutral. If the doctor earns a very good living doing this, his financial gains would be considered acceptable because the value of continued life is so great. If this campaign is to be successful, the universal neutrality of democracy and its cluster of rights must be established in a way that allows these symbols to become a part of the body of human kind. Within such widespread legitimization, their protectors would be readily granted the exceptionality they need to achieve goals they cite as being necessary.

When it comes to political power, no element is more vital than positive recognition and there is no better avenue for gaining positive recognition than through association. Whether this association is between individuals or countries, real power can be gained when one term or theme is automatically associated with a cluster of power-enabling and meaning-giving relationships. For Western nations, democracy fits all these requirements. Its cluster of terms and accepted meanings, when associated with certain sets of events, allows for the identification of the West as the sole interpreter, arbitrator, and protector.

The power of the term "democracy" lies in its historic association with other terms recognized over time as having developed in the West and then cradled and promoted by Western nations. However, democracy is not open to singular interpretation. Democracy, as understood and practiced, has gone through several development phases. Contrary to the current assumption that culture and politics are separate entities, democracy developed as a cultural and political system through centuries of conflict. Indeed, democracy's credited inception has its roots in cultural and political change: "The beginnings of Athenian self-rule coincided with Solon's liberation in the sixth century B.C. of those who had been 'enslaved' to the rich."[3] The direct democracy of Greece flourishing between 450 B.C. and 322 B.C. has, over the centuries, worked its way through a variety of incarnations and into its representative form found in Western nations today. In fact, it is "only in the closing decades of this century that democracy has been (relatively) securely established in the West and widely adopted in principle as a suitable model of government beyond the West."[4]

The nature of democracy is demonstrated in its historically experimental nature: "From beginning to end Athenian democracy was an experiment; no precedent, model, or outline existed to offer guidance."[5] And even today, democratic forms of government are as different from one another as they are similar. "After 2500 years of refinement, there is surprisingly little consensus on what 'democracy' actually means. One-party states, 'people's democracies,' socialists, capitalists, liberal democrats, republics and constitutional monarchies all claim, often vigorously, to be democracies."[6] But no current forms are really recognizable in Athens' terms. While the term "'democracy' . . . entered the English language in the sixteenth century,"[7] the current use of the term—as promoted by the West—really refers to Western liberalism. Bhikhu Parekh explains Western liberalism in these terms: "The view that the individual is conceptually and ontologically prior to society and can in principle be conceptualized and defined independently of society . . . lies at the heart of liberal thought and shapes its political, legal, moral, economic, methodological, epistemological and other aspects."[8]

Suppose, via time machine, our Athenian friends were to come to a Western nation to evaluate the performance of Western democracy in terms of Athenian democracy. First, the visitors would find no sense whatever in granting "self-determination" or political participation of any kind to people who did not follow their definition of "citizen." *So-called* universal suffrage would not be comprehensible to them. Neither would they understand representative government. They would find little sense in one citizen sending another to state his opinion. After they were around a while, they would find that the representatives are not delegated; they are not commanded to do the will of the people who elected them. The representatives, from the day after election forward, make their own choices. In the end, the Ancients would realize that Western liberal democracy is really an opportunity to vote for government management personnel.[9]

This is not to say that the Athenian form of government was better than the many divergent forms of democracy in existence today. Rather, it is to point out that forms of government are as cultural as they are political. The struggle for the Magna Carta was specific to a place and to a people—England and the English. It did not necessarily relate to the development of other Western democracies. Ironically, it was a feudal struggle. Like any struggle for power, it developed over a long period of time and in terms of a particular culture with its unique dynamic of political, economic, and social change.

Long after King John gave in and signed the document in 1215, the letter and the spirit of the agreement evolved along with the cultural assumptions of the time and through the push and pull of individuals and groups striving for change. It took six centuries of indigenous change for Anglo-American law to develop into its present form. It is still changing and being reinterpreted in light of new cultural perspectives. Democracy was not born as a system of no taxation without representation, of the right to a jury trial, or any other rights enunciated by the American colonists in the mid-eighteenth century.[10] These rights evolved after a considerable amount of social and political time. Yet these are now all firmly embedded in today's democracy.

But the market democracy campaign presents democracy as a political entity that should be achievable in a few short years, preferably within the time span of an International Monetary Fund (IMF) loan. We are supposed to assume that such change can occur without cultural implications. After all, it is a neutral procedure, a way of managing the people's government. What is wrong with such precipitous urgency? Isolating political forms from cultural facts artificially separates decision making from its rich undergrowth of culturally derived experiences. Herein lies a very real danger to the promotion of democracy as an attractive form of representative government. Democracy is attractive to so many of the world's people because it does offer freedom of expression about how their lives will be governed. Yet when democracy is being manipulated as a term and used as a Trojan horse to carry Western cultural assumptions and Western agendas, it loses its attractiveness. Because democracy has been denied its inherent flexibility to grow out of any culture and is tied, as a political system, to the culture of the West, it will be perceived as just another colonial effort. Its character, as an effective means of involving citizens in the governing of their own country, will be distorted.

This is not to attack democracy. As a form of government, it may turn out to be better than most. Framing it in proper indigenous context may in fact help countries develop more stable institutions that may serve to protect them from coups and saviors. But with democracy having now become a fetish placed beyond local referents and associated meanings, the term is an ambiguous cue word offering the experience of freedom for people in all sorts of roles, from consumer to citizen. Like other symbols, democracy has become a port of entry for underlying concepts without their being recognized as inherently adverse to the local culture in any real way. In daily interactions with Western transnational news and program narratives, the developing country citizen is becoming educated. Many already recognize the foreshortened cue and its positive associations without recognizing the cultural or often countercultural implications of these terms.

Grasping the essential thrust of this campaign will require a certain persistence in looking for things not said as well as those widely broadcast. This effort will require a scholar's determination, a businessman's street sense, and a politician's feeling for the slight of hand. Beyond such a sharpened focus, there is a need to break through the blur of such terms presented over and over in a certain politically manipulated context.

In every human being, words signal and cue one another with as much energy directed at leaving out detail as presenting and locating it. Words can activate associations with an entire history of thought but, in fact, cue only already known terms and experiences and communicate only the barest portion of that history. The test of the ideologist lies in his ability to select, shape, and communicate terms that create favorable recognition and association. In this perspective, the ideologist's lack of concern for the historic accuracy of a statement is readily apparent. To this bureaucratized intellectual, differences of "direct democracy" versus "representative," "delegated," or "guided" democracy are only important in citizenship courses or in settling intellectual argument.

Once the events and actions associated with collective memory are known, language and meaning are simply "there," available for manipulation. In the case of power of a third kind, language and meaning can be used to replace indigenous frames with events-associated frameworks constructed from outside. If certain kinds of events and responses to those events are positively connected to the established framework, the bureaucratized ideologist deserves his annual bonus. Such recognition and association between the designated terms, actions, and a particular identity can be filled with the power to control change. This, even if not one more democracy is established nor one more person's "human rights" is assured.

THE POWER OF INSTITUTIONALIZATION AND VALIDATION

The power of language is often spoken of in its semantic, word-to-fact function. Less often is the power of language used to offer its resources as intentionally created ambiguity. If there were only one kind of democracy, there might be a need for an enforcer, but there would be very little need for a judge or for validation of the use of the term. The magic and the power of politically manipulated terms lie in their ambiguous character.

Once the "market democracy" term has a certain manipulable recognition, association, and ambiguity, the final element of power lies in the Western institutionalization of the term into the plans and procedures of established organizations. Institutions are both overestimated and underestimated. They are overestimated as places for solving problems and underestimated as sites from which power to control change can be drawn. The fact that people are meeting in the same place, like the fact that people are communicating across the globe, does not mean that problems will be less likely to occur or more likely to be solved. Yet institutions can make a tremendous difference in the global contest for exceptionality by activating the process of a particular discourse without regard for the success or failure of the project. Understanding this difference between process and project is vital in making the rationale for exceptionality more transparent.

Such an understanding begins with a more realistic image of the political element behind the facade of bureaucratic neutrality. There is a core dynamic that typifies all institutions, beyond differences in their membership, stated functions, and operations. Institutions derive, initially, out of a consensus around how to handle certain situations or problems. Once institutionalized, however, the problems become forgotten and the institutional solutions become a living thing. As the institution grows, its procedures change to fit the power base of those most invested and most dependent on its continued success. In this process, the primary function of a mature institution shifts substantially from its original task of comprehending a situation to that of maintaining its own survival. By so doing, it clutches its most important power, the power of validation. Establishing its validity allows the institution to respond to those in control by offering their services as gatekeepers and licensers. In a way that is barely discernible, solving the problem is largely set aside in favor of bureaucratic roles as validators and keepers of the process.

All of this happens incrementally over time. There is no need for high-profile narratives of capitulation or selling out. The bureaucracies' collective memory of the institution's original intent is replaced by policies and procedural additions and amendments occurring from event to event in response to the perceived needs of the major investors. All this is accomplished under the assumptions of bureaucratic neutrality. Strangely, everyone knows that institutions function on the currency of self-serving objectives and common dependencies. Yet they seem to feel more comfortable assuming that bureaucrats are neutral, repeating narratives of self-denying altruism and public service.

The IMF and the World Bank are excellent examples of mature institutions where "weighted" voting power controls decision making. Increasingly, the interdependence between investors and those bureaucrats dependent on the institution becomes ever more evident in the way decisions and procedures respond. When IMF and World Bank officers apply the new "get democracy" and "get free markets" lending criteria, deferential and discretionary power is accorded to the validators by controlling members. Ironically, this ambiguity allows exactly the kind of discretionary decision making that Western law, from the Magna Carta forward, was established to foreclose.

A non-Western country on the receiving end of the discretion inherent in all this bureaucratized ambiguity has no standard by which to gauge real or imagined progress toward market democracy. In fact, democracy is far more ambiguous than the referents relating to Western concepts of progress in economic development. Then it was assumed that development according to stages would "naturally" lead to democracy—a notion now largely discounted. This also was a time when the West was eager to sell its technology and technical assistance to those developing countries being pushed to complete the objectives of development.

Now, with some developing countries actually in competition with the West for manufactured products and with the West restructuring away from low-transformation products to high value-added technology, the push for development has been placed far behind the Western nations' need to match the market strategy of Asia. The West does not need to develop more Asian-type competition for manufactured products. But the West is quite eager that developing countries supply the market with their raw resources—the more in the market, the lower the price for developed countries. The West wants "hungry, middle-class appetites" spending money earned from selling raw resources at inexpensive prices, not from being effective competitors with the West in value-added products.

It is easy to see the winds of change blowing through the bureaucratized minds of Western policy makers. Today, the agenda has switched from "getting into" development to "getting into" the market economy and "joining up" with democracy. The fact that getting into the market requires infrastructure for which there is no available financial support is another concrete fact not mentioned when selling the process of a market economy. In the heat of the Russian presidential election, one of President Boris Yeltsin's opponents looked directly at the world's television screens and said, "Get into the free market? That's impossible. We don't have any cash!"[11] Just how struggling nations should go about joining up and getting in is left for them to discover. What is not open to discussion is whether or not they will join the free market economy. The democracy and free market process are already so powerful that positive acquiescence to the project is assumed. Developing countries are only urged to make English more available to speed up the one-way communication.

In its derived and intentionally constructed ambiguity, the term "market democracy" not only sends a clear message of Western priorities, but ratifies the need for Western judgment and validation. In this position, the West can be both good cop and bad cop simultaneously. As timely as a program policy change between national media and a local station, the market democracy program becomes the central rationale of the United Nations, the World Bank, the IMF and, as it is turning out, a majority of non-governmental organizations (NGOs).

In his 1993 report to the General Assembly, former United Nations' Secretary General Boutros Boutros-Ghali insisted that "there can be no flowering of development without the parallel advance of another key concept: democratization."[12] Yet nearly every recent analysis finds no link between the establishment of democracy or any of its cluster of rights, and the success or even the onset of economic development. Most analysts agree that the only condition that indicates any particular relevance to the development of democracy is that of a positive transition. [13]

The idea that democracy leads to development corresponds, not coincidentally, with the inauguration of the market democracy strategy of American foreign policy. Just as international institutions resonated the deficit reduction, supply-side economic orientation of the Reagan administration, they now mirror the Clinton administration's democracy and markets focus. Again, once the cue terms gain currency and are clearly in the hands and intentions of powerful international players, their associated linkages and discretionary ambiguity allow them to be adjusted to temporary or long-term objectives and likely sets of events.

As the validation inherent in the priority granted these terms becomes a part of the procedure of the international organization, all potential and current players line up for evaluation and confirmation. Countries feel the pressure to become publicly identified with the term as it is pushed on them through institutional leverage, resonated in mass communications, and promulgated through various governmental and non-governmental conferences and meetings. Desperate countries simply cannot survive without the promise of powerful political and economic support. Therefore, they become living referents to the Western political terms being promoted. In effect, they need to be seen as having already bought into the association and the identification Western nations enjoy with these terms.

How easily all of this is done. Working under the umbrella of "leaders of the free world," where Western governments share funding for the much-needed jobs, developing countries' bureaucrats in international organizations happily propagate the policies of their employers, often at real cost to their home countries' interests. It is what is called a "win-win" situation. They are there, they are paid much better than they would be in their own countries, and their own countries are proud of them for being there. They know the language and they are necessarily respondent to institutionalized rewards to deliver whatever messages the system will allow. This does not mean that such hard-working people do not actually accomplish a great deal for their countrymen and for the global community as well. But it does mean that, given the potential for establishing a universal Western concept of Man and of human power already within reach of these dominant benefactors, they are providing public signature to these concepts.

This institutional resonation and validation carries an organic political momentum of its own. Not unlike a licensing function, every time the non-Western nations request validation, they are willingly granting Western institutions the kind of leverage essential for attaining and maintaining hegemonic power. Such a transaction grants the validator the purest form of institutional control. The symbolically promoted need is not obscure or hidden in some sort of conspiracy. Even pro-Western writers recognize its power, assuming it is benignly beneficial for the countries being granted the identity, not just the validator.[14]

This is the wonderful plasticity of language manipulated for political advantage. Institutions created to promote the good of all mankind—peace, growth, elimination of hunger, promotion of good health, protection of the environment—are institutions from which no nation can afford to be excluded. Failure to ascribe to these terms can stigmatize a nation, effectively putting it outside the gates of civilized international society. The process is rarely linear, but given the reach of institutions and electronic communications, the exponential dynamism of multiplying terms begins to accelerate. As the momentum builds, control centralizes and the hidden cultural assumptions behind the original terms become more transparent but, alas, much too late to be easily changed. The Western cultural underpinnings gain even more support from domestic constituencies whose education make the ideologically loaded symbolic justifications seem all the more logical. Both at home and abroad, in foreign countries and in international institutions, these terms begin to stand as pillars of global universalism no longer respondent to multicultural political facts.

Terms like "market democracy" become a sort of sacred totem, an international dividing line. If such a totem enjoys global consensus, a less powerful nation without a sanctioned form of democracy could lose its right to the assumption of sovereignty or accessibility to the legitimizing discourse of international organizations.

Discourse regarding the complexities of power of a third kind has revealed a kind of cognitive difficulty in understanding that, despite the stated purpose of a symbol or an institution, both can be used to mobilize meaning for a particularly manipulated purpose. For some reason, it is difficult for many thinkers to separate two kinds of analysis. One analysis involves looking at the people working within a system and toward an objective. Then there is an analysis of the way the system itself can be used by others for quite different purposes. The privatized media has the task of producing infotainment that is attractive to consumers and profitable for the corporation. That fact is only a fact, neither good nor bad. However, as a *system*, the media is available for use as a resource for people with intentions entirely unrelated to the media system itself. In foreign policy, Western nations' use media and international institutions to mobilize meaning in a search for exceptionality. Reporters work very hard getting out the news, but their work without their intention, is part of a system foreign-policy planners can use.

Unless a thinker can get out of the trap of being either a supporter or a critic of the actions of people within the system, he will never be able to see the system as a resource. This is especially true when evaluating the role of NGOs in foreign-policy making. Drawn by the good that these groups often do and the service they provide to many poor nations around the world, it is important to maintain the distinction between their actions within the system and the utilization of that system for attaining exceptionality. There is no more evidence of conspiracy between NGOs and government than there is between the media and government. If there is, that is the basis of another book by a different author. The need to maintain legions of people involved in doing good throughout the world requires thousands of professionals and billions of dollars. Those dollars can only come from people whose interests, in and out of government, coincide with the interests of a particular NGO. In the end, however, they are all selling their services for the funding they need to survive as bureaucracies. There can be no criticism here. This is the reality that gives our world the selfless men and women who dedicate and sometimes give up their lives helping people in desperate conditions in places like Bosnia, Chechniya, Rwanda, and the Congo.

Totally apart from the good that is done, however, it is important to take an unemotional look at NGOs as an emerging system: To what extent does the NGO system become a resource for the mobilization of meaning by Western governments using power of a third kind? Like the media, NGOs are searching for as much maneuverability as they can acquire, with as little resulting counterpower as possible. As they expand, their needs expand and meeting those needs stresses their persona as being neutral and altruistic. Because most of them find the majority of their funds within Western countries, they not only enter non-Western countries and go before the media with Western cultural assumptions, they select projects and represent positions corresponding to—or at least not deviating too far from—the values of their Western donors. In an era of power of a third kind, they fit perfectly.

NGOs: FOOT SOLDIERS IN THE DEMOCRACY AND FREE MARKETS CAMPAIGN

Once a marginal part of the international political system, NGOs have begun to emerge as major players with significant financial, informational, and political power. Functioning on slim budgets and largely locked into individual issues, the NGOs have found a solid niche in the widening gap between the erstwhile power of bi-polar rhetoric and the need for exceptionality. NGOs were traditionally seen as both independent from government and without many close connections with each other. They had long ago tailored their appeal for funds and legitimacy to the most simplistic narratives, narratives attuned to developed country governments and donors, their only site and source for funds. In one fund and membership drive after another, they had become masters at drawing the most compelling media portrayal of their ideological position and the plight of those they were organized to protect.

The political character of NGOs has changed dramatically over the past decade. Their incipient power, their structure, their impact on international relations in general, their incorporation into governmental foreign policy, and their impact outside of and within governments of the developing nations is badly in need of reassessment. Like intellectuals who entered the foreign-policy institutions after World War II, the NGO intellectuals have been brought in from the marginal, low-status position of independent "thinker" or "do-gooder" to the status of managers of institutions having a legitimate practical purpose. Even though they are "out there" in the grassroots, they are more than ever "in here" as a part of the establishment.

NGOs in 1994 enjoyed over 10% or $8 billion of worldwide public development aid, "surpassing the volume of the combined UN system ($6 billion) without the Washington-based financial institutions."[15] This financial power exists to the extent that "in 1992, NGOs provided $8.3 billion in aid to developing countries, representing 13 percent of development assistance worldwide."[16] In a 1990s atmosphere of cost-management, "the increase of donor-funded NGO relief operations and Western disengagement from poor countries are two sides of the same coin."[17] In 1993, "at the Social Summit in Copenhagen, Vice-President Al Gore committed Washington to increasing [the current allotment of 25% of US assistance channeled through NGOs] to 50% by the turn of the century."[18] No matter how lofty their ideals or how pragmatic their aspirations, the NGOs are increasingly attractive as an alternative means of carrying out aid and assistance programs that were traditionally the province of governments.

Coping with balanced budget requirements and recognizing the need to shift away from Cold War diplomatic and military structures, the United States State Department in 1993 proposed a reordering of defense, foreign affairs, and intelligence spending to conform with the rewrite of the 1961 Foreign Assistance Act proposed to Congress by the Clinton administration. The decision by State to persuade President Clinton and the Congress "to break down the so-called fire walls that separate defense and intelligence resources from the rest of the international affairs budget"[19] was closely mirrored by the lobbying strategy of NGOs in Washington. In the fall of 1993, they submitted a letter to President Clinton, Vice-President Gore, and other administration officials urging "an 'integrated international engagement strategy' to be financed by combining the government's defense, foreign affairs and intelligence budget accounts." President Clinton received that same letter with signatures from 140 additional NGOs from around the world.[20]

Indeed, the Clinton administration wants "to integrate the work not just of government agencies but of international voluntary organizations and of U.S. universities and hospitals with programs overseas." Being "inside," the NGOs would be in a position to "participate in 'the policy and program planning process.'"[21] Presumably, they could also become a part of the State Department budget categories, "promoting U.S. prosperity," "promoting sustainable development," "building democracy," and "promoting peace" as well as "providing humanitarian assistance."[22]

Funding, however, is not the most significant part of the NGOs' eagerness to fit within United States foreign-policy decision making. With only 400 NGOs registered with the U.S. Agency for International Development (required in order to qualify for U.S. government grants) out of the 1500 NGOs registered with the United Nations for observer status,[23] money is not all they're looking for. Julia Taft, president of InterAction, an umbrella organization for 150 U.S.–based nonprofit organizations working in 165 countries, said at the time of the 1993 budget discussion that "we're the ones who are out there working internationally, but without the U.S. government's leadership, we're out of business." Collectively, her members receive seventy-five percent of their funding from private sources. Vitally important is U.S. commitment to a foreign policy that relies on what the NGOs have to offer.[24]

And it is not just the American government with which the NGOs wish to develop an institutionalized symbiotic relationship. While NGOs are attracted to government signature and funding sources, so too are international organizations attracted to the foundation funds, personnel, and expertise that NGOs can access. The United Nations Habitat Conference, held in Turkey in 1996, used NGOs to organize and fund-raise for the event. United Nations' representatives were clear when they thanked the various NGOs for their help: If the NGOs had not taken up funding the conference, the United Nations would not have been able to hold it.

All this cross utilization of funding and personnel brings up the critical question of NGO independence. The reality is that they are no more independent than media corporations. They are private, non-profit, issue-based organizations in heavy market competition for a zero-sum pot of funds. Where media must garner the viewing time of consumers to sell to corporate advertisers, NGOs—if they want to maintain the generosity of government and support of multinational grant-giving institutions—must become a legitimate and demonstrable part of government and institutional strategies. A study of human rights NGOs found that

> access and effectiveness [of human rights NGOs] depend on deliberate policy choices related to NGO goals; skills and professionalism of staff; resources devoted to UN matters; informal relationships developed with UN personnel, independent experts and diplomats; and, in turn, the successes of the organisation and other nongovernmental organisations in building new UN mechanisms to respond to the inputs from NGOs.[25]

Human rights groups increasingly find themselves supporting United Nations missions, agencies, commissions, and even individual members. They give not only information, advice, and visibility, they also provide staff: "Human rights NGOs will probably continue to be the principal sources of personnel for future UN human rights monitoring missions." Indeed, "today, [they] seem on the verge of being offered the prospect of becoming 'insiders,' working through and with the UN to achieve what has not been possible or desirable for them in the past—the delivery of legal services."[26] As the United Nations' budget constraints and restructuring efforts proceed—and as NGOs successfully lobby to become formal "members" of the institutions they now observe—the availability and willingness of NGOs to fill the gaps can only mean significant changes in policy and priorities within the organization.

Still today, the informal role of NGOs is powerful enough. NGOs, numbering 176 in 1909[27] and over 15,000 in 1995, use so-called "internal modes" of promoting their agendas, including "pressure on a government to participate in a treaty-making effort; formation of domestic coalitions and the mobilisation of public opinion to influence the positions a state takes during treaty negotiations; public pressure on a government to sign a treaty; and using the strengths and weaknesses of a country's domestic system to challenge governments, companies and others to comply."[28] Externally, they spend their efforts "urging the United Nations or one of its associated agencies to add an issue to the agenda; gathering data to help frame or define a problem or a threat in ways that influence the work of official UN-sanctioned conferences; and contributing to the implementation of treaties by assisting countries without expertise to meet their obligations."[29]

These external modes are becoming more and more institutionalized: "In 1993 . . . 30% of [World] Bank projects had provisions for NGO participation" and "the UNDP [United Nations Development Program] has changed policy over the last decade so that local NGOs are receiving allocations in the Indicative Planning Figures (IPFS) that used to be exclusively reserved for governments."[30] Especially important is small state use of NGO personnel instead of their own representatives. They know that co-opting a delegation allows exceptional access. As a Greenpeace attorney explained: "The value of even just one 'friendly' small state if that state's representative is . . . scientifically trained, well-informed, and co-operative, for that person not only has the automatic right of access to committees and working groups, but also, in the one-country, one-vote system [of the General Assembly], has the same formal power as any other state, however large its delegation."[31]

Herein lies the access to power via proxy that literally no national entity can get except through leverage or implied threat. Taking a well-tutored representative in hand, they move, in effect, from the hallway and the lobbyists' lounge into the role of de facto "voting member." NGOs are nearly irresistible to some developing nations. In exchange for de facto proxy power given them by NGOs, countries' representatives gain increasing amounts of funds and widening influence and connection with political and economic centers of power. Faced with so many issues of immediate domestic importance, exchanging one's vote seems a small price to pay for the aid or connection afforded by an NGO representative. But it is not just the developing country that is co-opted into the NGOs' strategies, the NGOs themselves have been co-opted. For the developing nation representative, this co-option has become such an ordinary fact that it was hardly noticed when the American government's delegation to the Rio conference included supposedly independent NGO groups.[32]

In the end, these *non-governmental* groups are very much *governmental* groups without the usual nettlesome, costly, and time-consuming problems of accountability and bureaucratic screening. As one worried critic put it: "Influence without accountability is also dangerous; and it is not easy to see how voluntary organisations can be made accountable, and to whom. Above all, in the nature of things, it is the richer organisations in the richer countries that will have a predominant say; and while this cannot be helped, it should certainly not be encouraged either."[33] This quasi-governmental position allows NGOs the flexibility that governments do not enjoy. So they become a resource for governments. For example, in the early 1980s, Central America became an area of Cold War importance. "Between 1980 and 1987, aid spending tripled in the [Central American] region, 15 per cent of it provided by and through NGOs. European governments, opposing US policy but not wishing to confront the US directly, channelled additional money through NGOs. . . . As one observer put it, 'only two institutions have consistently flourished in the Central American crisis: the military and the NGOs.'"[34] Yet another analyst described it this way:

> Ultimately, there is a question as to how much the "civil society" discourse and donor infatuation with NGOs has to do with democracy and human rights, and how much it has to do with finding cheaper and more efficient alternatives to faltering governmental delivery systems. . . . *By squinting hard, NGOs can be seen and treated simply as contractors, just another private sector alternative to government in general, and to bad government in particular.*[35]

Another indication of NGO political power is the response of organizations opposing the opinions espoused by the traditionally liberal NGOs. One such group is the National Rifle Association (NRA), one of the most powerful American organizations lobbying the United States Congress. The NRA recognizes the institutionalization of NGOs within the United Nations and their growing influence not only within developing nation governments, but increasingly within the American government. Their 1997 decision to organize as a lobbying organization at the United Nations is an acknowledgment of a new reality. The anti-gun policies promoted by certain NGOs currently providing "information" to the United Nations' members could create policies incompatible with their position, positions that the United States government might endorse.

NGOs: Looking Beyond Project to Process

NGOs are excellent vehicles for the use of power of a third kind. As willing, and often unwitting, foot soldiers for Western policy planners, they reflect the same systematic centralization of elites seen among Western foreign-policy intellectuals. They function within the same Venn diagram of networks, where all the circles of government, international corporations, the media, and ultimately the citizen/consumer intersect with each other. They appeal to the world's largest economies for financial resources, and spend the funds on themselves and in the countries of "the Rest." Their value system, their simplistic narratives, and their zealous rationale for action find a home in the Western "market democracy" construction so dominant at this century's end.

So the work of NGOs on the part of and at the behest of the governmental and issue-centered institutions is more than mere rhetoric, inflated symbols, or "doing good." NGO power would be real power in any age, but in the current vacuum of definition and amidst Western efforts to fill that vacuum, the NGO system is a perfect fit. In effect, it is a well-funded definition and validation machine. Its primary function is to redefine and reshape Western concepts and narratives and communicate them with the promise and the threat of NGO intrusion into events.

Nor are the NGOs new to the process of narrative intrusion into events for a targeted result. While enjoying the use of all their purportedly neutral and objective images, their fund-raising approach is familiar to those represented in the preceding chapters. By making "use of news events and media coverage, which raise public awareness in a way that no paid advertisement could ever achieve," they capably attract funding; "the more dramatic the event, the greater the media coverage, and the greater the ease of fundraising around it."[36] Unlike governments, however, they do not have to struggle for exceptionality or worry about reciprocity.

The NGOs role in all of this Western mobilization of meaning is not just an add-on. It is essential. NGOs are the nodal links in a worldwide network of constructed and constantly promoted and communicated discourse. The NGO professional is the messenger, the shaper, and the promoter of Western culture, pointing to the faults of wrong-doers. News reporters on the scene are too costly and are limited by their need to appear objective. The NGO professional is a highly educated, articulate replacement of the reporter. He is a representative of Western elite culture, "on the spot," recognizable as "one of us," and eager to make a presentation pleasing to his governmental and institutional donors. He is also on the scene, able to speak English, and because he looks like "us," he will be trusted to be objective but within "our" own cultural value positions. He is a roving actor ready to enter the play, trained by the best and the brightest of Western liberal academics, certain to have the right script and to speak clearly enough so the people in the back rows can hear and understand.

Taken in terms of a longer view, NGO professionals are actually intellectuals-in-training, future bureaucrats needed to manage the global village. In fact, if the campaign toward establishing market democracies and saving the planet does not pick up speed in terms of global acceptability, the personnel for the new global bureaucracy may be ready before they are needed.

The NGO and Human Rights

NGOs have been the chief lobbyists of human rights from their first statements in the United Nations charter. Due largely to their efforts, the United Nations has a Human Rights Committee made up of representatives of those 113 countries who have signed The International Covenant on Civil and Political Rights. Referring to the need to have international monitoring of the human rights of states, a legal commentator on the work of the Committee writes, "Now that the inhibitions of Cold War politics have been lifted and the liberal democratic sensibility is widely shared by the membership, what began as review by politicized, anticolonial committees of the General Assembly and by the Trusteeship Council may be expected to become a judicious process of principled rule interpretation by independent experts."[37] Because "arms have been devalued, the relative international significance of influence over the media, of money[,] . . . of the ability to collect, marshal, and disseminate information, and of claims of representivity has grown, and NGOs hold vast collective accounts of each, clearly surpassing those of many states."[38]

As a concept, human rights began as an NGO effort promoting a single point of view and ended as a recognized committee in the United Nations, steadily working to turn that principle into a standard measurement subject to international monitoring. The NGOs' aura of neutrality and representative altruism, combined with their associative and access power, is an advantage they press continually. Thus, it is true that "because NGOs can push harder and more openly for more drastic changes, which can then be codified over time by the UN, *a 'symbiotic' relationship has developed in the context of establishing new human rights standards and implementing existing ones.*[39]

Like the West with "democracy" and "free nations," NGOs have had some success in identifying themselves with the values they pursue. Just as democracy is, first, a Western-created vehicle tailored for the tasks involved in governing a nation, human rights is thought of as a vehicle for giving people a better life or a better way of life. Democracy has already been pushed from vehicle to a goal on its own. People are not told to *use* democracy, they are told they must *have* democracy. Without democracy, they are seen as living in *inhumane* conditions. Human rights also is being turned from a vehicle into a goal. Once it is a goal with universal value, its actual effects will not be as important as whether one *has* human rights. At this point, it becomes a fetishized commodity to be acquired and, simultaneously, a fungible political currency usable in exchange for all sorts of political and economic advantage.

In all this, of course, the definition of human rights is left to the NGO representatives. With the term "human rights" already being used as criteria for judging a nation's worthiness to participate in vital financial and political relationships, one expects to find definitional agreement equal to that of the time honored term they are working so hard to replace. The history and scholarship behind sovereignty is remarkable for its probity and for over three centuries of development in actual political situations. But none of this is apparent when one talks with NGO representatives at their conferences. They stand in the hallway thoroughly frustrated with the way the nation-states get in the way of the global community. For them, the world began just after the Cold War. To them, people defending their sovereignty are simply locked into an irrelevant past. Meanwhile, the NGO professional, firmly grounded in both the fast-fading present and the constantly changing future, bravely defends the individual against all such anachronistic national forces.

To these urbane travelers, culture exists entirely separate from national politics and national sovereignty. Multicultural means the anthropologically noted differences between humans. How does this impact, then, their definition of "human rights" as a term the NGO is so eager to have replace the three hundred-year heritage of the term "sovereignty"? What will replace the single conceptual consensus upon which the world currently makes life and death decisions in trying to maintain a semblance of order? The emotion-filled aspirations are there, but these representatives of human rights as a value and as a goal "by no means reflects common agreement about rights questions, as illustrated in June 1993 at the UN World Conference on Human Rights in Vienna."[40]

The NGO and Ecology

Ecology is nearly equal to human rights in its ability to be turned from a term into a vehicle for power. However, it is much more effective and apropos than human rights to the task of creating pro-Western assumptions granting exceptional global access to resources and markets. Because issues of ecology necessarily involve access to resources and their use, this access-to-markets effort defines the nation-state as the problem. With rising awareness among the leadership in developing countries regarding the relationship of raw materials to national participation in the global economy, the nation-state will assert that resources within their boundaries are their resources. Not only will they say, "Our resources belong to us," they will also say, "We can do with them what we will." This is certainly a reasonable statement from a sovereign nation, but not what commercial, governmental, and non-governmental elites from developed nations can afford to hear.

In this decade, the pinnacle moment of symbolic action presaging shifting definitions of terms came at the 1992 United Nations Conference on Environment and Development held in Rio de Janeiro. Here, the theme of "risk" was used to give a clear indication that the territories of the South belong to the world and, without global oversight, the "world's resources" would not be adequately protected for all the people in the global village. The stage was set for the justification to intrude in the "ecology"—not the nation—of any country. The most significant battle was the right of a nation to its own resources, to use those resources for the benefit of its people without the globalization of national development by universal environmental principles.

Consider the area of gene technology, the resource issue that will dominate the twenty-first century. Currently, "medicines from plants are worth about U.S.$40 billion per year." In one instance, "a single gene from an Ethiopian barley plant has been used to protect California's U.S.$10 million annual barley crop."[41] The 1972 United Nations Conference on the Human Environment addressed biodiversity issues for the first time. Actually, it did more to highlight the developing nations' naïveté regarding developed nations' disregard of a nation's sovereignty over its natural resources. In 1983, the United Nations Food and Agriculture Organization passed a non-binding Undertaking on Plant Genetic Resources. Under its provisions, "access to genetic resources should not be restricted, and it declared that all seed resources were the common property of humanity. Both primitive stocks and those developed by proprietary means should be free to all."[42] Developing nations accepted the language, assuming it meant little because it was non-binding; besides, they were hopeful of attracting aid to meet the provisions.

By 1992 and the Rio Conference on Environment and Development, aid had not been and was not going to be forthcoming, and biodiversity was the subject of a non-binding Undertaking on Plant Genetic Resources, signed in 1983, that all seed resources belonged to all peoples on the planet. When the developing countries arrived in Rio, they were much more aware of the implications of what they had signed and no longer concurred. In 1991, the National Biodiversity Institute, a non-profit Costa Rican research center, signed an agreement with Merck and Company, the world's largest pharmaceutical company, for a U.S.$1 million up-front fee and royalties.[43] A nation's rights to its indigenous resources did gain stronger language in Rio where the biodiversity convention acknowledged a nation's right to negotiate access on terms of mutual agreement.

However, the issue is far from resolved. So important was the issue of intellectual property rights in the area of genetic engineering that "the U.S. led a campaign to prevent retrospective claims by Third World countries to earn royalties from the commercial exploitation of indigenous plant species."[44] In fact, the ultimate decision by the United States *not* to sign the accord was centered around the unresolved issue of intellectual property rights. The United States' position was that access to and transfer of intellectual property rights would be "on freely negotiated, mutually agreed terms that recognize and are consistent with the adequate and effective protection of those rights." More importantly, they argued that "the sharing of benefits derived from the use of biological and genetic resources are understood to be without regard to the sources of such resources."[45]

Very little basis for agreement was realized over who would fund the costly NGO dream to "protect the integrity of the global environmental and development system" while "*recognizing* the integral and interdependent nature of the Earth, our home."[46] Indeed, the Agenda 21 Agreement reflects the developed nations' opposition to global funding to protect the "global environment." Published following the Rio conference, *The U.S. Fact Sheet: Agenda 21 Agreement* was clear: "The proposals in Agenda 21 reflect a balanced approach toward finance and emphasize the need for developing countries to rely primarily on their own internal resources. . . . In its approach toward finance, the United States stressed the importance of favorable domestic economic conditions, the role of the private sector and the need for innovative methods, such as debt-for-nature swaps."[47]

There was no success in the general effort of the developing countries to link their concerns with debt relief, technology transfer, nondiscriminatory environmental practices and standards, and improved terms of trade, and the developed nations' agenda of climate change, rational forestry management, preservation of biodiversity, and provision for toxic management. Again, to Western NGO environmentalists, or better, preservationists, this was an environmental not a cultural or political problem. Despite the incredible cultural, political, and economic impact on developing nations of the biodiversity effort at Rio, the NGOs and the West followed the same strategy in separating cultural questions from political and economic questions.

Like so much of the NGO work, the entire Rio conference was definitional. It was an attempt to mobilize a particular set of meanings and to form a global consensus around those meanings. It is important to separate process from project as do NGOs and foreign policy ideologists. The project is stated as "cleaning up the planet" on the developed nation/NGO side, while "development" was the watchword on the side of the developing nations. This is what the press reported. But power of a third kind operates on a process, not a project level, and the process at Rio was definitional, not material.

All of this may seem cynical. Maybe it is. However, that does not change the necessity to understand the NGO system as a process for mobilizing a certain set of meanings and frameworks compatible with Western goals. Yes, it is necessary for the world to get together to "clean up the planet" and to adequately house the world's people. Many NGOs are admirable in their pursuit of often lofty ideas and the performance of admirable acts of assistance to humankind. Such a response is a prima facie requirement in a world made smaller by population growth and technology. However, we are not talking about the project, we are talking about the process; and more specifically, about the terms of discussion and the character and syntax of international discourse. If conferences on the environment and habitat continue in a political culture of monologue, then the conferences have a single objective: to provide the pretext for usurping the sovereign right of "the Rest" to the possession and use of their resources. In effect, they create a culture of monologue that broadcasts a single point of view. Repeated often, that single perspective can become the central point of departure for global discourse and, ultimately, decision making.

NGO bureaucrats are not just administering or even implementing policy. They are auxiliary players in the making of consensual definitions globally compatible with developed nation's foreign-policy objectives. With their access in both the developed and developing countries, and with their special status in international institutions constantly improving, they are the only lobbyists with real effectiveness in organizations like the United Nations and the World Bank. The meetings and conferences they host offer excellent rhetorical terrain for a network of people who, mostly unknowingly, are engaged in a sophisticated effort to mobilize meaning for their own position and, through them, for the much more expansive power of those funding them.

Like the advertisers, media, and foreign-policy and political professionals, NGOs are part of a tight sociology with much more consensus than conflict. Even the cross-fire of supposedly contradicting forces from the left or the right are often more a matter of complaints or disagreements over technique in what is, fundamentally, an intellectually shaped centrist policy orientation. They rarely quarrel over questions of cultural or human effect. The developed nation intellectuals—in-house and NGO—are projecting a foreign policy that is shaped to make the most media-positive impact in the short term while constantly repeating long-term themes, narratives, and identities equally positive in creating Western "world brand" presumptions.

Thus, the NGOs and intergovernmental organizations are rendered to the level of access/resources for the institutional projection of government foreign policy. That may or may not be their direct intention; nevertheless, the results of their efforts are resources for the mobilization of meaning on the part of governments. In particular, human rights and "save the planet" programs fit the criteria for Western foreign policy perfectly. They allow the nearly unlimited "right" of the West to enter, isolate, or condemn any country in order to "protect" global rights, human or ecological, as per Western ethnocentrically loaded constructs. It is an attempt to elevate certain kinds of political choice and actions beyond the power of every nation except a few Western nations. It places the acts and the events surrounding these choices within those Western narratives that describe the appropriate ways in which individuals and nations ought to make choices.

So, for the Western nations, it all comes down to sovereignty and what to do with it in the more complex world of the late twentieth century. The term "sovereignty," despite its three-hundred-year-old vintage, is as vulnerable to change as when it was created at the end of the Thirty Years War in Europe. Consider that the Westphalian Treaty of 1648 explicitly responded to "the rejection of some kind of transcendent, *supra-national* moral basis to political authority" and established that "states are sovereign and possess their own intrinsic moral authority; as such, it does not require any kind of moral agreement beyond the recognition of differences."[48]

Despite this clear statement, the nature of words in times of intense competition is such that irony rather than consistency can be depended on. Today, the ironic "logic" is apparent to the point of absurdity. On one hand, sovereignty, and specifically its non-intervention principle, was and is meant as "a positive defence of the integrity of the sovereign state as the framework for individual freedom, respect for rights and individual fulfilment."[49] On the other hand, there is a human rights campaign intended to abrogate sovereignty in order to protect individual freedom, create a respect for individual rights, and to establish individual fulfillment. Even more absurd is the fact that the most powerful standard bearers of human and individual rights are themselves engaging in a policy intended to make sovereignty utterly porous on the grounds that the world needs the West to act as "supra-national moral authorities."

Understood in all its sophistication, this new campaign reaches into the institutionalized political culture of nations. This campaign will work within local process without raising factual questions. In every nation, opposing forces mediate within culturally articulated institutions and common understandings. These are the screens and the parameters for negotiated actions between competing individuals and groups. In terms of the effects of this campaign, these screens and parameters are the most fundamental and the most threatened element of indigenous cultures. Even when only partially successful, the attempt to universalize political process trifles with centuries-old processes for managing, mediating, and implementing differences of opinion, goals, and objectives. Responding to the agendas and mobilized meaning of their boards of directors, Western and non-Western bureaucratized professionals create a kind of disconnect between indigenous processes of judgment and local peoples. If not diagnosed in time to create an effective strategy, this bureaucratic distance can be lethal to the integrity of the nation's decision making.

A successfully universalized assumption that the Western form of political process is the only "true" system and, in any case, the only one that actually protects the rights of the individual, threatens to create a devaluation of a nation's indigenous institutions. In terms of international relations, power, change, institutions, and ethnocentrism are all brought together by the electronic wonder of communications. When understood as processes that will be lifted from their traditional moorings and wrapped around the instrument of electronic communications, power of a third kind emerges in all its awesome potential. To comprehend that power, observers will need new perceptual models. These models must be constructed to allow non-Western peoples to see power in new forms, to comprehend change in new realizations, to see through the way institutions can be made to serve new functions and, finally, to recognize the far-reaching uses of ethnocentrism when it is elevated to a universal neutral premise.

Power of a third kind and the entire process of creating culturally transcendent frames is very difficult to define or even to clearly discern. This process is incremental in its development and respondent to no known time table or clear evolution. It is not an announced conflict with clear stages and results. In actual practice, this supra-national campaign does not pose a vote or no vote, democracy or no democracy decision. People do not meet to decide whether the Western vision of political choice is the right one for all nations. In fact, meetings are created and processes are orchestrated to make certain such a question does not arise and that no one is called on to make a clear public decision. When that is accomplished, the global village will have been colonized.

Projects are concrete, arguable; process is only to be found deep in the structure and the flow of interactions. They are at a level where people are so inside of their institutionalized assumptions that it is difficult to even shape the kind of questions that make form and directions transparent. After all, how does one discern such phenomena as the lifting of a nation's intricate mosaic of decision making and governing from a nation's cultural history? This kind of campaign is more like guerrilla warfare than a declaration of war. One just awakens to find that, without knowing it, war has been going on for some weeks.

The entire campaign to erase difference and conflict requires that as little difference be noted as possible—all within an ambiance of no conflict whatever. The campaign and its objective depend on the separation of politics from culture to the extent that political actions do not occasion cultural conflict. Once culture and politics are separated, it becomes possible to say: In all matters and events excepting the individual's relationship to the nation, the response must be based on a nation's own cultural history. When dealing with issues that impinge on the rights of the individual and the individual's relationship to the nation, people must strive to reach for the Western definition and the Western process and, if necessary, Western protection.

The tactic for this campaign is as old as persuasion itself: To establish an assumption as being beyond question, you must allow as few opportunities for critical questioning as possible. This is why analysis of this colonization effort must penetrate beyond individual issues and projects to the level of making process transparent. While Western academics busy themselves deconstructing political and social constructs and methodologies and reshaping them for political clients, non-Western intellectuals need to move from post-modern critique to post-insular critical thinking. Effectiveness in the era of power of a third kind lies less in criticism of Western thought than in comprehending the ability of Man to use global media access to interpose himself into once insular communication and interpretation. These efforts at comprehending the use of power of a third kind require that non-Western intellectuals *"explicate the connection between the meaning of symbolic constructions and the relations of domination which that meaning serves to sustain."*[50]

Non-Western nation intellectuals must not only aggressively participate in this era of power of a third kind but must create a sophisticated discourse based on concepts derived from non-Western cultures. Non-Western intellectuals need a new language of power, change, institutions, and ethnocentrism notable in the way such newly integrated codification differs from their colleagues in the Western world. A re-codification of global discourse with new parameters, procedures, and understandings will not and cannot be done outside the highly dynamic and interactive global discourse suddenly so much a part of everyone's way of life.

Recodification is no longer an entirely insular matter to be dealt with on the level of individual projects, issues, or personalities. Nor is it a matter of pouring over text or engaging in word-splitting discussion. It is a pragmatic effort with significant political implications. It begins with the strength of local cultures actively mediated within the demands and complexities of a newly shrunken global village.

The intellectual communities of East and West are entering a period of intense negotiation and persuasion, cooperation and conflict. Nothing less than the allowable parameters and imaginative limits of human thought and action are on the table. Looked upon critically, most cultures are filled with resources for confronting and articulating these parameters. Why not, then, visit those horizons to present their nations in a more favorable posture, one which the world understands and accepts today? Yet many people in the developing world are not quite able to comprehend the massive watershed of interpretive, imaginative, and communicative change coming down upon them in this, the end of the twentieth century.

A question: Without the intentional propagation of Western concepts of Man by a dominant culture, would developing countries, left on their own, absorb the terms "human rights," "democracy," and "self-determination" and would they accept them as justifications for transgressions of sovereignty? Probably not. In any case, as long as the West has a need to control change, there is no chance in this post-insular world that any nation will be left alone. There may be widespread indifference to their needs, promises made today and forgotten tomorrow, but they definitely will *not* be left alone.

NOTES

1. Anthony Lake, "The Four Pillars to Emerging 'Strategy of Enlargement,'" excerpts from a speech given at the School of Advanced International Studies, Johns Hopkins University, Baltimore, 22 September 1993, *Christian Science Monitor*, 29 September 1993, p. 19.

2. Michael Stopford, "Locating the Balance: The United Nations and the New World Disorder," *Virginia Journal of International Law* 34 (Spring 1994): 697, quoting U.S. State Department, *Presidential Decision Directive 25*, May 1994.

3. Cynthia Farrar, *The Origins of Democratic Thinking: The Invention of Politics in Classical Athens* (Cambridge, England: Cambridge University Press, 1988), 7.

4. David Held, "Democracy and the New International Order," in *Cosmopolitan Democracy: An Agenda for a New World Order*, eds. Daniele Archibugi and David Held (Cambridge, England: Polity Press, 1995), 98.

5. Harvey Yunis, *Taming Democracy: Models of Political Rhetoric in Classical Athens*, Rhetoric & Society series (Ithaca, N.Y.: Cornell University Press, 1996), 3.

6. Ian Smillie, *The Alms Bazaar: Altruism Under Fire—Non-Profit Organizations and International Development* (London: IT Publications, 1995), 216–17.

7. Ibid., 216.

8. Bhikhu Parekh, "The Cultural Particularity of Liberal Democracy," in *Prospects for Democracy: North, South, East, West*, ed. David Held (Stanford, Calif.: Stanford University Press, 1993), 157.

9. Ibid., 165.

10. Louis Menand, III, "Human Rights as Global Imperative," in *Conceptualizing Global History*, eds. Bruce Mazlish and Ralph Buultjens (Boulder, Colo.: Westview Press, 1993), 179.

11. *CNN WorldNews*, 24 May 1996.

12. Boutros Boutros-Ghali, *Report on the Work of the Organization from the Forty-Seventh to the Forty-Eighth Session of the General Assembly* 2–3 (New York: United Nations, 1993), quoted in Stopford, "Locating the Balance," 687.

13. Baohui Zhang, "Corporatism, Totalitarianism, and Transitions to Democracy," *Comparative Political Studies* 27 (April 1994), 110–11.

14. For a discussion of validation, see Thomas M. Franck, "The Emerging Right to Democratic Governance," *The American Journal of International Law* 86 (January 1992): 46–47.

15. Leon Gordenker and Thomas G. Weiss, "Pluralizing Global Governance: Analytical Approaches and Dimensions," in *NGOs, the UN, and Global Governance*, eds. Thomas G. Weiss and Leon Gordenker, Emerging Global Issues Series (Boulder, Colo.: Lynne Rienner, 1996), 25.

16. Peter J. Spiro, "New Global Communities: Nongovernmental Organizations in International Decision-Making Institutions," *The Washington Quarterly* 18 (Winter 1995): 49.

17. Rakiya Omaar and Alex de Waal, *Humanitarianism Unbound?* Discussion Paper No. 5 (London: African Rights, November 1994): 6, quoted in Gordenker, "Pluralizing Global Governance," 25.

18. Gordenker, "Pluralizing Global Governance," 25, quoting "NGOs and Conflict: Three Views," *Humanitarian Monitor* 2 (February 1995): 32–33.

19. Dick Kirschten, "Crisis Prevention," *National Journal,* 11 December 1993, p. 2944.

20. Ibid.

21. John M. Goshko and Thomas W. Lippman, "Foreign Aid Shift Sought By Clinton," *Washington Post*, 27 November 1993, sec. A, p. 1.

22. Kirschten, "Crisis Prevention," 2943.

23. Andrew S. Natsios, "NGOs and the UN System in Complex Humanitarian Emergencies: Conflict or Cooperation?" in *NGOs, the UN, and Global Governance*, eds. Thomas G. Weiss and Leon Gordenker, Emerging Global Issues Series (Boulder, Colo.: Lynne Rienner, 1996), 68, quoting AID 1994 Annual Report, *Voluntary Foreign Aid Programs, Bureau for Humanitarian Response* (Washington, D.C.: Government Printing Office, 1994), 70–97.

24. Kirschten, "Crisis Prevention," 2945.

25. Felice D. Gaer, "Reality Check: Human Rights NGOs Confront Governments at the UN," in *NGOs, the UN, and Global Governance*, eds. Thomas G. Weiss and Leon Gordenker, Emerging Global Issues Series (Boulder, Colo.: Lynne Rienner, 1996), 58.

26. Ibid., 63–64.

27. John Agnew and Stuart Corbridge, *Mastering Space: Hegemony, Territory and International Political Economy* (London: Routledge, 1995), 193, citing M. Zacher, "The Decaying Pillars of the Westphalian Temple: Implications for International Order and Governance," in *Governance Without Government: Order and Change in World Politics*, eds. J. N. Rosenau and E.-N. Czempiel (Cambridge: Cambridge University Press, 1992), 65.

28. Gordenker, "Pluralizing Global Governance," 39, quoting Lawrence Susskind, *Environmental Diplomacy: Negotiating More Effective Global Agreements* (New York: Oxford University Press, 1994), 50.

29. Gordenker, "Pluralizing Global Governance," 39.

30. Ibid., 31, quoting World Bank, *Cooperation Between the World Bank and NGOs: 1993 Progress Report* (Washington, D.C.: World Bank, 1993), 7.

31. Spiro, "New Global Communities," 50, quoting Kevin Stairs and Peter Taylor, "NGOs and Legal Protection of the Oceans," in *The International Politics of the Environment: Actors, Interests, and Institutions*, eds. Andrew Hurrel and Benedict Kingsbury (Oxford, England: Clarendon Press, 1992), 130.

32. Spiro, "New Global Communities," 50.

33. I. G. Patel, "Global Economic Governance: Some Thoughts on Our Current Discontents," in *Global Governance: Ethics and Economics of the World Order*, eds. Meghnad Desai and Paul Redfern (London: Pinter, 1995), 33.

34. Smillie, *The Alms Bazaar*, 228, quoting David Lewis, cited in Kees Biekart, "European NGOs and Democratisation in Central America: New Policy Agendas and Assessment of Past Performance" (paper presented at IDPM Workshop, University of Manchester, June 1994), 3.

35. Smillie, *The Alms Bazaar*, 237. Italics added.

36. Natsios, "NGOs and the UN System," 71.

37. Franck, "The Emerging Right to Democratic Governance," 60.

38. Spiro, "New Global Communities," 48.

39. Gordenker, "Pluralizing Global Governance," 29, quoting Ramesh Thakur, "Human Rights: Amnesty International and the United Nations," *Journal of Peace Research* 31, no. 2 (1994): 143–60. Italics added.

40. David Held, "Democracy and the New International Order," 115.

41. Marian A. L. Miller, "The Third World Agenda in Environmental Politics: From Stockholm to Rio," in *The Changing Political Economy of the Third World*, ed. Manochehr Dorraj (Boulder, Colo.: Lynne Rienner Publishers, 1995), 253, quoting Mostafa Tolba, *Earth Audit* (Nairobi: UNEP, 1972), 15.

42. Miller, "The Third World Agenda," 256.

43. Ibid., referencing the World Resources Institute, *World Resources 1992–93* (New York: Oxford University Press, 1992), 130.

44. Mark F. Imber, *Environment, Security and UN Reform* (New York: St. Martin's Press, 1994), 99.

45. "U.S. Statement for the Record on Agenda 21 and the Authoritative Statement of Forest Principles, June 14, 1992," *Foreign Policy Bulletin* 3 (July/August 1992): 49.

46. "Rio Declaration on Environment and Development, June 14, 1992," *Foreign Policy Bulletin* 3 (July/August 1992): 49.

47. "U.S. Fact Sheet: Agenda 21 Agreement," *Foreign Policy Bulletin* 3 (July/August 1992): 45–46.

48. Raymond Plant, "Rights, Rules and World Order," in *Global Governance: Ethics and Economics of the World Order*, ed. Meghnad Desai and Paul Redfern (London: Pinter, 1995), 191–92. Italics added.

49. Ibid., 193.

50. John B. Thompson, "Mass Communication and Modern Culture: Contribution to a Critical Theory of Ideology," *Sociology* 22 (August 1988): 372.

CHAPTER 5

Power of a Third Kind: A Role for Developing Nations?

From the first light of human intention on this planet, the genius of imagination has created ever more awesome extensions of human capabilities. From this vortex of thought and technology, new systems of human interaction replace familiar parameters with new roles, rules, and rituals.

Of all such creations, none have the sweeping social and political impact of electronic communications, especially television, its most ubiquitous creation. No matter what is done, from impotent attempts at censorship to sophisticated programs for creating critical understanding, a global culture is emerging. Grasping power of a third kind and using it in this process to the advantage of ones own culture will be as natural as all other human uses of power. The only question is who will control the inevitable process of shaping and defining this global culture.

Western nations have already gained a rudimentary grasp of the systems and process of turning electronic communications into the tool it is for power of a third kind. This book has demonstrated the early uses of this power in their campaign for "market democracy." The only question remaining is the willingness of non-Western nations to step into this historic momentum and become an equal partner with the West in defining the global culture. The range of responses are as wide as any human choices and the impact as potentially dangerous as any wrong step.

Doomsday responses are not appropriate. Despite the Western nations' commitment to the campaign, one must not assume that it is a sure success or that all are in complete agreement on its form and implementation. The entire effort is just being debated and tentatively rehearsed on the world stage. These countries and their intellectual elites are still in a process of conflict and cooperation, and they do know the difficulties of developing a thoroughly effective strategy. They know the history of trying to create permanent institutions based on unchangeable ideologies. They know that power and change flow together from seemingly permanent patterns only to suddenly separate into barely recognizable shapes with seriously unintended consequences and counterpower. The triumphal rise and the demoralizing eclipse of once powerful individuals, institutions, and nations is an all-too familiar tale.

Western nations' elites also know that events coagulate into trends and thence into insurmountable obstacles at out-of-control speed. In fact, there is increasing concern among Western planners that time may run out on the attractiveness of Cold War exchanges and understandings before the global mobilization strategy is realized. Communications advantages in transportation are in such a state of rapid and often unpredictable transformation that planning and strategy are often outstripped. Stretched for time and resources, but standing alone in the ability to physically access people in every corner of the planet, Western nations can still use their international institutional power to realize their intentions.

Developing nations' intellectuals should not underestimate or overestimate the institutional power of core Western nations. Neither should they underestimate the way these institutions have become globally transparent. Playing both sides of the political street when the whole global village is floodlit requires more skill than ever before. Until the early 1980s, gentle nudging and hallway trade-offs in international organizations could be done within the comfortable certainty that confidences would be kept and, even if they were covered by the media, they would be given very little exposure. However, as was proved by the conflict over a second term for former United Nations' Secretary General Boutros Boutros-Ghali, institutions have become as transparently non-insular as nations. Back rooms have suddenly become global living rooms filled with millions of educated viewers.

America's exertion of power in its 14-1 vote in the Security Council to oppose Boutros-Ghali was given the highest possible media coverage. The counterpower was evident in the vocal challenge over American control of the United Nations and the bickering between the United States and France. This is exactly the kind of coverage Western nations can least afford. This fact of transparency is the primary venue for the occurrence of counterpower that will have potential every time institutional resources are stretched to gain supra-national exceptionality.

COUNTERPOWER, EXCEPTIONALITY, AND RAGE

This book was written on a single strategic assumption: Once developing nations' intellectuals are committed to the critical task of making the Western ethnocentric global mission transparent and intelligible, a counter strategy can be formed. That strategy could result in freshly developed visions for a non-Western politics of choice, allowing multiple visions from multiple cultures. There also would be a chance to undercut the Western assumption that development is only possible if all nations adopt the Western political process. The entire effort must successfully attack the assumption that non-Western political systems cannot function peacefully within a global international framework. That effort must put the underlying logic of universal Western political process under sharp scrutiny.

There are two kinds of counterpower, one leads to rage, the other to incompetence. In the first instance, counterpower occurs when the actions of individuals or groups break through the boundaries of those understandings accorded consensual acceptance. This kind of counterpower happens when, out of actual need or as a result of sheer ambition, an individual or a nation acts in ways that go beyond the consensus or even the recognized spirit of social or political understandings. In simple terms, people say, "Look, we understand the need to strive for advantage but this action is unacceptable." When this happens, individuals respond with rage. Rage is the public externalization of the perception that the boundaries of allowable action have been intolerably breached. Thus many argue that the rage in America toward the actions of the United States government in Vietnam or the rage of the people of the former Soviet Union to governmental action in Afghanistan occurred because people were not made ready for the actions these governments took.

With the full vision of hindsight, foreign-policy pundits now claim there was a need for intensive reinforcement of such mobilizing frames among national constituencies. The understandings of the political and military elites were remarkably synchronized. But the framework was not well established in the minds of significant sectors of the American or Soviet Union polities so they could integrate events and actions in Vietnam or in Afghanistan.

In the breach created by widely divergent discourses, both nations were rocked with counterpower. They had created a schism between the expected and realized ways constituencies viewed acceptable governmental alternatives. In effect, these elites had breached the tolerance of their peoples' understanding of purportedly justifiable action. Rage was the result. The permissive exceptionality normally granted foreign-policy decision making was withdrawn as being generally unjustifiable. The market democracy campaign is an attempt to make people ready for a global Western culture. Planners can only limit the rage generated by the loss of cultural and political alternatives if favorable cultural themes reach the level of global assumption.

In the second instance, the refusal or unwillingness to use power creates the context for counterpower. This is because the refusal to rise to the level of conflict undermines future power positions vis-à-vis maneuverability and the increased demand for resources. This is so because both the exertion of power and the reaction to that exertion find their source in subjective human interpretation and communication. One does not just lose the present battle in terms of the objectives of the aggressor. In effect, by not participating, one has lost position when one turns to face the next conflict.

Consider inaction regarding sovereignty. Suppose, having determined that its interests are not materially affected, a nation takes no action over a transgression of sovereignty in another country. Or suppose that a nation becomes signatory to a convention or treaty that affects the sovereignty of others when that treaty has been crafted to exclude any direct impact on itself. Time moves on and power of a third kind only gains ground by being ignored. Later, when its own sovereignty is being tested, that nation finds that its ability to respond has been reduced. Now there are new requirements and new resource demands for rising adequately to the conflict. The level of conflict originally necessary for maintaining sovereignty has been fueled by the lack of response. The once safe nation is forced to work within a new context where maintaining the assumption is much more demanding.

Refusal to respond to the Western attempt to impose meaning on events and actions is as far-reaching as the over-exertion of power. Human beings always strive for order on their own terms. Because they are necessarily opportunistic, no situation is left without meaning or without some attempt to impose meaning on events, conditions, or situations. Wherever and whenever a single human being acts in terms of other human beings, no vacuum can exist. As a distinct form of human striving, communication is rhetorical and political. From imagination, to interpretation, to interaction, communication is a subjective process done in terms of the likely response of others. Every exertion of power is necessarily mindful of the inevitable consequence of some kind of counterpower. This transactional view of power means that every moment that the market democracy campaign moves forward without a non-Western response, a high wall is built around the ability of non-Western nations to protect and project their own culturally derived political process.

The equation for the counterpower currently mounting against the West is resident in the campaign effort and in the current context of that effort. As stated earlier, the more powerful the nation, the more it needs maneuverability. The more maneuverability needed, the more exceptionality for action is required. The more exceptionality demanded, the more its actions must be seen as neutral and altruistic. The more that their actions are required to be neutral and altruistic, the more constrained the nation is in its transnational actions. Such an inversion of perceived power and the mitigating fact of greater vulnerability to counterpower existed long before power of a third kind. But with global transparency, the traditional alternatives of the most powerful nations are further depressed and undermined. This electronic transparency has altered the entire idea of power by virtue of the fact that smaller nations with fewer demands risk less counterpower.

In essence, new forms of power create differences. These differences are the windows into the future of global political life. Intellectuals must pull back the curtains and look through that window. Once done, they must communicate it to each other and to their nations' citizens. Stating that power always shapes itself to its most powerful vehicle is not so profound. What is truly profound and useful is being able to show how that power is used, and how it is evolving and changing. If an aggressive program for altering the site, substance, and participatory levels of global discourse is to be accomplished, intellectuals' analytic involvement and active mediation are a minimal requirement. The site for that involvement and mediation is in the dynamic space between the exertion of power and the realization of counterpower.

EXCEPTIONALITY FROM SOVEREIGNTY: POWER AND COUNTERPOWER

The key strategic component in Western global efforts to create culturally transcendent frameworks is the trivialization of power, change, politics, and culture. This strategy of trivializing has one serious flaw: it represents Man and human process as they are not. Beyond the inherent falsehood of this representation is the fact that its historical context is one of high transparency. Not only has electronic communications created a window on the world but nearly everyone in the world—Western and non-Western—is looking through it. The facade of universality being wrapped around Western concepts is already vulnerable to such widespread transparency. The tensile strength of the entire symbolic structure is weakened further when its underlying warrants are seen as a set of false representations of human kind and human process.

The West is reaching for a situation in which the global community would ask where the individual would be without Western liberal democratic culture and how it would survive without Western nations' protection. Establishing such a framework is highly susceptible to significant instances of counterpower. No matter how lax in enforcement or twisted to fit a narrow agenda, a rule, any rule, is a baseline that involves constraints and burdens for all those submitting themselves to it. This means that by making market democracy the rationale for exceptionality, Western nations must only transgress the sovereignty of nations that are not democratic or not a free market. Any action taken by a Western nation against a non-Western nation outside that rationale will be attacked on the grounds of a still accepted sovereignty principle. Ironically, the more successful the campaign is in actually establishing democracies, the more limited the rationale will be for intervention.

Similarly, a refusal to respond to any attack on democracy and the free market will be seen as cynicism and a failure of resolve. In a less transparent world, Western nations could gamble that omissions of this kind would not be a part of public knowledge. Given the need for such wide margins of exceptionality, nearly any expectation will be a trip-wire for Western nations. Already the complexity of their situation is so great that they have had to create the Group of 8 (G8) in order to get away from the restrictive arena of real international participation. Now, global transparency will betray supposedly neutral actions as actually self-serving.

If it is to succeed, the market democracy platform needs to establish Western actions as neutral. Neutrality is what allows a judge to maintain his credibility and keeps a protector's motives above suspicion. It takes years to establish the premises and image of Western nations' being a neutral actor in world affairs. This is time the market democracy planners do not have. In a political arena of non-Western participation, counterpower from precipitous action in this single area could unhinge the entire campaign.

The Need to Use Power of a Third Kind Before It Is Ready

There is already counterpower potential in the need to use the market democracy rationale before it is ready. Ill-advised or inept use of power of a third kind will undermine the already shaky perception of Western nations as neutral and supra-moral, supra-national entities. The credibility of Western nations also will be threatened by their inevitable default on such expansive promises brought on by a lack of ability and adequate resources.

Precipitous use of the democracy interpretative frame for leverage is more a statement of the strength it does *not* have than the power it *must* have to meet the stringent requirements for Western exceptionality. Being forced to use power of a third kind before it is ready can create counterpower at home as well as in the global village. Because of this, the transparency that threatens to weaken institutional leverage will have the same effect on the establishment and use of the market democracy strategy.

Maintaining the image of protector overseas risks running afoul of domestic constituencies and budgetary constraints. Because domestic considerations were a key reason for the market democracy campaign in the first place, this is a serious risk in counterpower. For example, President Clinton's signing of the Helms-Burton Law helped win Florida's electoral votes, but only one month later this successful effort became an international problem. The democracy theme was serviceable as a face-saving means for American and European policy makers, but it meant bringing the democracy interpretative frame into international service before it was ready.

During the Cold War, foreign policy in Western countries was more constituency-permissive in the sense that leaders were given the benefit of the doubt under the assumption that they know something citizens cannot know. Now, with the full knowledge that decision makers themselves watch CNN and respond to it, the viewer begins to feel that he knows enough to have a well-tutored opinion. This transparency has stripped the mystifying distance from the face of decision makers and has made once easily dismissed events into issues that must be comprehended within policy making. Without the televised bomb in the Sarajevo market, would the United States have become involved? Probably not. Without the televised picture of American soldiers being dragged through the streets of Somalia would American troops have been pulled out? Probably not. Without the image of French soldiers chained to posts in former Yugoslavia, would the French have agreed to a coalition force? Maybe not.

Once they place themselves as watchmen, everything that happens on their watch will require an explanation and a justification. Domestically, stretching resources and risking lives for democracy or free markets—as backing away from human rights has shown—may find a somewhat hardened constituency. The more successful the market democracy campaign, the more the lack of response will earn counterpower among both domestic and global constituencies. Western commitment to these heavily promoted but dangerously ambiguous frames will be threatened by the realized counterpower of lower and lower credibility.

Using democracy and human rights requires an unbiased relationship to terms that are supposedly neutral and inherent in being human. They must not be perceived as transparent vehicles for hegemony. The impression that these terms are being used in entirely cynical and self-serving ways could unhinge the investment in these terms, their inherency, and the identity of the West as protector and judge.

More Demands Bring Greater Restrictions and More Counterpower

During the Cold War, propaganda programs bent toward swaying individual countries were adjusted to the indigenous national political cultures in order to gain acceptance of Western military action. Military action is no longer a singular strategy. Rather, it is a tactic within the strategy of the post-modern promulgation of universal themes. In this new strategy, communications and military technology are turned into vehicles for the establishment and, ultimately, the use of the market democracy interpretative framework.

Here the ambiguity of the market democracy umbrella experiences its first stress of negative international reaction. Military coalescence in individual instances of turbulence is accomplished only with a great deal of difficulty. But coalescence in the ideological posture of Western nations, each harboring different market and political goals and pressed by quite different constituency demands, is a challenge of an entirely different order. Coordination and concordance is truly a daunting task when the enemy is ambiguous or case-by-case. This is especially so when the objectives, rationale, and strategy are often incompatible and subject to deferentially chosen goals and objectives. The struggle to expand the North Atlantic Treaty Organization (NATO) within such circles of ambiguity is an early example of the task ahead for Western nations attempting a common front without a common enemy.

Counterpower inherent in such strategic demands already is quite clear. Since the Cold War ended, economic and constituency constraints require that military power be used only within coalitions of other nations. Being policeman of the world was a great enough source of negative domestic constituency reaction. But being police*man* has changed to the demand that these Western nations be police*men*, collectively presiding over an increasing number of internal and border conflicts. Again, non-insular transparency plays the role of catalyst for a nearly endless number of vulnerabilities and conflicts. This is so even when military action had to be approached with an eye turned toward constituency reaction and the trip wires of other strategic dependencies.

Conflict between France and the United States as to which country should lead NATO's Southern European theater of operations was a part of this continuing saga. As individual nations, decision makers would like to use military power and other forms of leverage to deter other major powers or to keep weaker nations in line. In a world constantly on CNN and BBC, the requirement that more than one nation be involved in all conflicts restricts the use of leverage to its most subtle and largely ineffectual forms. Televised news forces decisions in place and timing not necessarily in tune with an individually initiated, carefully planned strategy, let alone when a coalition is required.

As power of a third kind begins to play an ever larger role in global foreign policy, individual nations will compete for the use of reported events and the benefits deriving from that use. Doing well by doing good can be an arena of competition over who has done the most good and who most deserves to do well. There has already been evidence of friction between France and the United States over who deserves greater advantage from work done in the former Yugoslavia and Africa. After the Gulf War, the conflict over who should get more contracts and more arms deals at the expense of war-weary treasuries was so offensive that even apolitical people in the area were talking about it. The Cold War Brezhnev Doctrine divided up the world into well-defined territorial spheres of influence. That has been replaced by the assumed rights of competing developed nations to symbolic spaces where all want to be the hero. For example, are Rumania and Albania European countries, to be protected by other European countries, or does such turbulence require the United States to intervene as universal protector of democracy? Is the protection of democracy and individual rights open to any nation capable of convincing everyone else that they are right for the role of the protector?

On a political level, it may be a coalition effort but, as leading Western nations have never really denied, the primary objective is markets. How long will Western European countries be willing to sail along in the wake of the democracy/human rights campaign if, like France in Yugoslavia, they took all the early risks to deal with internal turbulence and find that they must still compete with the United States for contracts afterward? Ideology has been used to control and gain access to markets before. But can the same ideology be used to gain markets when the nations using it are fierce competitors for the same markets? The counterpower in this coalition effort is already evident in the international upset of France with the United States in Africa and, in particular, on the Security Council. As France and Germany begin to deal with the economic restructuring so upsetting among American and British constituencies over the past decade, they will be even less likely to go along with the kind of exceptionality that ends in the United States picking up all the economic marbles once the turbulence has subsided.

Under these conditions, how can a Western front be presented with enough coherence to make the market democracy campaign achieve its objectives while meeting so many different agendas? In these early days of power of a third kind, the campaign will stumble over the entangled trip wires of resource scarcity, constituency demands, and international constructions. And given the need for markets, coalesced or national actions will lay bare contradictions within the supposed neutral posture of Western nations. In effect, the objective of establishing global frameworks seems more realizable and less challenging than the capacity of Western nations' domestic elites and coalitions to effectively use them.

Unintended Effects of the Premature Use of Counterpower

Until power of a third kind comes into its own as a mature way of imposing and mobilizing meaning, Western nations may find that its premature use has created a volatility within the expectations, perceptions, and actions of the global audience. Use of power of a third kind to create an order that fits Western agenda can be expected to increase the complexity and unpredictability inherent in promoting that agenda. Because Man is constantly altering his vision and response to the world, it would be naïve to assume that the absent audience would remain a passive participant in the use of power of a third kind. Expectations and perceptions among the global audience will affect the speed with which they assume problems should be solved. Then, as they watch the benefits gained by Western nations in the use of power of a third kind, the global audience will try to affect national events through their own activation of Western narratives.

Timing is so rapid and the benchmarks of judgment are so out of space that global absent audiences are much less permissive toward the world's leading nations. Ironically, the success of television involving everyone in the action has resulted in audiences becoming accustomed to the time and space syntax of episodic news. Then, when these minute-to-minute scripts give way to the same narratives presented within half-hour dramatic scripts, it must be expected that viewers as citizens would ask, "Why are they going on and on? Haven't we already solved that problem?"

The new global citizens' demand for simple answers, quick responses, exciting new issues, and problems amenable to more simple narratives increases complexity and narrows response options. These deep structure changes have little to do with specific policies of a given government. But when political leaders are just as impatient as their constituents with anything but a case-by-case response, something important has occurred. That something could well be the demise of grand theories and grand foreign-policy strategies and positions in favor of in-and-out policies and actions.

If this were not enough, the global citizen can quickly become savvy to uses of power of a third kind. When the Serbs took to the streets to demand Slobodan Milosevic's acceptance of election results, the signs they carried were all written in English. They knew their real audience was global, not local. This is true now of almost every event in which the domestic component appeals to the global audience. It is no longer enough to focus on changing the minds of the people at home where their lives are still largely time and space bound in the immediate present. Any appeal also must be made to the absent audience of which they are a part. When you are part of the global absent audience, becoming a part of presentations of the global electronic discourse is more important than being part of the local one. An act of civil disobedience in Serbia aims for the constituencies of Western nations' leaders, not local leaders. A revolution in former Zaire confronts local leaders with no interest or conception of how to appeal to constituencies of Western leaders. This is so even when those Western leaders will be acting as intermediaries in vital peace negotiations. Zairians are not yet a part of the global absent audience. They still present their global protest in their local language.

In effect, unprecedented use of this unprecedented power of a third kind will have results as unpredictable as they are unintended. Not all unintended results will be positive to the market democracy campaign. Under the right conditions, perspectives and expectations resulting from the exertion of power of a third kind can be volatile and filled with counterpower.

POWER OF A THIRD KIND FOR THE NON-WESTERN WORLD

Developing nations' intellectuals must abandon the role of disgruntled camp followers of yet another intramural competition over forced choices. Promising and exciting intellectual work is the result when they step outside the thinly scripted role of worthy opposition to Western thought and actually begin constructing their own ways of looking at power and change.

Despite a plethora of seminars and conferences, institutes and publications, intellectuals of the East and the West have allowed their thought to become a part of two campaigns running on parallel tracks. On one track, Western intellectuals have become bureaucratized into the petty dreams of politicians' electoral strategies. On the other, their non-Western counterparts massage the threatened egos of those who assume that the best way to protect culture is not to question your own, while you joyfully tear another culture down. Meanwhile, other intellectuals on both tracks are trying to ease out of their role as apologists for status quo political demands while distancing themselves from petty cliques. Unfortunately, there are so few of these latter thinkers that their thought is read only by other disenchanted intellectuals communicating in contrived meetings and ever more marginal communicative organs.

Developing nations' intellectuals have the opportunity to grasp the shape, systems, and dynamic of this use of power of a third kind in ways that actually surpass the understanding of those using it. Because use of this new power is only just emerging, its outlines and ramifications are only beginning to show themselves. As we have seen, this is particularly true in foreign policy. While the availability of response time for developing nations' intellectuals is increasingly a problem, there is still ample opportunity to create a strategy to comprehend and conceptually communicate power of a third kind and the way it is being used.

There also is an opportunity to shape a long-term strategy that will go beyond defense to focus on the elaboration of non-Western constructs where success depends more on what they offer than what they counter. At a minimum, this effort includes the implementation of a vision that can motivate their counterparts in all countries toward the use of a more globally positive power of a third kind.

Developing nation intellectuals must take the role of mediation more seriously than was necessary in an insular time. They must intervene between the involvement of their fellow countrymen as members of the globally projected "absent audience" and their involvement as everyday citizens interacting within an indigenous culture and nation. To do this well, they must form a sophisticated understanding of power of a third kind.

In every country, the primary mediation must be the burden of the parent working within the family. But as a result of the penetrating power of the media, parents are only marginally better equipped to cope with the inundation of symbols and images than their children. Monitoring and censorship are answers from the past and only partially comprehend the future. Mediation in the era of power of a third kind demands the timeless value of critical thinking. Because it goes to the subjective source of all human power, critical thinking is the only effective intervention in the non-insular conditions created by global electronic communication. Use of and training in critical thinking in the school and in the home must be done as part of a seriously intentional effort to prepare for a non-insular future. Without this response, global communications will serve as unfettered channels for the culture-laden narratives of Western ethnocentrism.

The movement toward critical thought is, unquestionably, *global*. Sudden alterations in the range of experience for once insular peoples could occasion a new chance for openness and a new site for advancing the understanding of different points of view. Power of a third kind could end in a new awareness of other cultural and political viewpoints and a new sensitivity to the logic and derivation of other ways of looking at the world. Unfortunately, the West is committed to using power of a third kind to make its narrative the story of the history of all peoples. The West is prepared to invest in that realization and to stake its credibility on the universality of that narrative to a point that actually outreaches its own conviction in it.

In the terms of this more reflective age, when one talks about "watershed political change," one means that the stories meant to narrow the ways of understanding the world—the ways common sense should look at and discuss that world—are being rewritten. A new script is being tossed around and made ready for global use. It is the shaping of that script and the systems created to establish its universality that must be the focus of the developing nations' mediation and recodification efforts.

This entire effort becomes more clear when seen as an intentionally shaped process. For example, most intellectuals would argue that the most far-reaching fact of this period is the utter destruction of distance. Yet developing nations' intellectuals still subscribe to the Western Cold War/post–Cold War definitions of change. What is more germane is that this is now a post-insular period. When they accept "post–Cold War" as the definition of this new era, it masks the fact that a quantum change in alternative exertions of power has occurred. Western assumptions shape non-Western questions so that the answers come back within Western constructs. Unwittingly, developing nations' intellectuals perpetuate age-old political narratives that place the perception of change within a Western political agenda.

An adequate response will not be arrived at easily. And in any case, that response will have to be as strategically provisional and adaptive as the policy itself. What will *not* work is more readily apparent. Nothing will come of making Western nations or their policies a source of widespread moral attack. While it is always important to point out hurtful strategies and actions, falling into the swamp of easy cynicism is a non-response to change. In the era of power of a third kind, there is a demand for a more actively critical analysis. Telling the same story over and over is the least effective way to comprehend transitions in power and change.

Developing nations' intellectuals must comprehend the hidden relationship between political discourse and political intention. The ideologists' primary goal in competing discourses is to limit the choices and the questions to be asked about a set of actions. By narrowing the range of alternatives, they create forced choices. Once done, the ideologist works toward limiting the range of alternative justifications. At a certain point in the effective mobilization of global political discourse, attacking a narrow set of answers creates its own trap.

No matter how much one attacks Western culture, if that project is in that culture's terms, subsequent international discourse is controlled by the West. Thus there is no real advantage and a great deal of vulnerability in joining the discourse of democracy–no democracy. This question masks a more important one: What is the relation of culture to political process? If one stays within this forced choice discourse, one trivializes the complexities of concepts enriched by hundreds of years of intensive interaction. That heritage involves complex issues of values, assumptions, and unique individual perspectives derived out of a particular human and physical ecology. Such a trivialization replaces this complexity with the assumption that democracy–no democracy involves only the willingness to choose it. Human rights is another issue where its complexity is trivialized. The reality is that human rights are a problem in every country and the refusal to deal with a people's right to a meaningful life is not only wrong but, in the end, involves significant counterpower. If an answer equal to the complexity of this issue is to be found, however, it can only be found within the cultural system of a given nation.

Human rights is not exclusively a Western invention. The Muslim world knew it more than fourteen centuries ago when, as the Quran says, "we have honored the sons of Adam." On this all encompassing principle, a whole series of what is today considered the core of Western liberal individualism could be constructed. To honor a human being is to respect the inviolability of his life, his family, and his property. To honor a human being is to respect his right to free choice, his freedom of expression, and afford him an equal opportunity to actuate himself.

The best way for the developing nations to contribute their dogma to human civilization is by first implementing it within their own societies, thereby removing the need to import foreign assumptions. What is happening in many developing countries today is not so much the absence of cultural sophistication as the absence of modern instruments to implement that sophistication.

Thus there is a need to actively search for an altered vision of present occurrences and trends. Such a defense of divergent political process requires a critique of the way developing countries seek out solutions to problems and the way they evaluate these solutions. Western foreign policy strategies depend on weary but still vital formulations in a discourse where the same words continue to be said in somewhat the same manner and by the same people. Even the same postures are being taken. But there is a critical difference in the project when the *process* is different. Buoyed by nearly universal access to global decision makers, power of a third kind can be used to trivialize traditional cultures, institutions, and political choice. Once done, the West is able to interpose its political objectives into the indigenous political process of non-Western nations.

TOWARD A CRITIQUE OF DEVELOPING NATIONS' THINKING

How prepared are non-Western nations for meeting the demands of such a power-backed and power-filled effort toward establishing a global political process? How ready are they to participate in the creation of a global culture? In general, they are not that well prepared. They are far too committed to a culture of monologue that limits their alternatives.

First, many developing nations' intellectuals too often assume that what has worked in the past will necessarily be the best solution to present problems. When intellectuals turn away from the present and future in their search for answers, they cannot see the entire enterprise as part of a significantly altered process. This dependence on first premises distorts the primary role of the intellectual as mediator, relegating him to the position of biased apologist and political historian. A new attitude toward the role of mediator is needed. The intellectual's contribution to the welfare of his own people depends on two parallel perceptions about the past. To the extent that experience can be used to clarify and understand the present, reference to the past is invaluable. However, to the extent that the present and future are forced to fit the experience of the past, the intellectual's commitment to the past becomes counterproductive.

Second, most developing nations' intellectuals will admit that a society that seeks real answers to real problems must maintain an attitude of critical evaluation. But the facts of their discourse tell a different story. From the school room to the boardroom, an assumed protocol betrays a determination to exclude critical interrogation into the deductive and inductive processes behind statements. Too often, they are not probative regarding the evidence supporting this or that position. The unwillingness to question the collective memory of tradition or to get beyond the cult of personality are only instances of intrinsic failure so much a part of a culture of monologue.

Third, developing nations' intellectuals favor a discourse obsessed with personality. In searching for answers, they try to ignore asking "what" and "why" and even "how," and, instead, ask "who." Too often, they are in search of this or that leader of supposedly historic proportions who will become the new soothsayer, ready and able to lead them out of the darkness. This personality cult has not only paved the way for dictatorships and tyrannies, it has enabled such oppressors to present themselves as the only way out of distress into salvation.

Finally, the discourse of developing nations' intellectuals has gotten so used to the monologue of spectator they do not realize they are affirming and even promoting positions directly harmful to the future of their own people. At home, at school, inside companies, and in international conferences, developing nations' intellectuals communicate the assumption that a passive, uncritical response to change is favored over an attitude of skepticism. In this era of power of a third kind, such a response virtually guarantees a future where non-Western nations become more and more a part of the periphery of history.

If non-Western intellectuals merely dance from one event to another in tune with Western orchestrations, they will never have their own projects, let alone their own process. They will suffer the fate of the counterpower that derives from inaction. Knowledge as global education and knowledge as propaganda already typifies Western communications to non-Western countries, resonating and justifying further political intrusion. Without effective mediation now, future developing nations' intellectuals will be identified with the parental admonitions of Western nations.

In the end, non-Western countries will be made all too willing to grant exceptionality from rules that will continue to bind all others. Were they to question their own patterns and processes, they would come to prefer the easy path, accepting already proven Western constructs rather than build their own from the storehouse of ideas in their own cultures. This is why it is so difficult to understand the carefully wrought constructs and concepts projected by their Western counterparts. Caught in an endlessly repetitive web of outdated deductive thought, wittingly or not, they court the counterpower of incompetence and a future of limited alternative responses.

Clearly, time is running out on the opportunity to develop a response equal to the level of conflict. If non-Western nations were already alerted to this power of a third kind in ways that create an effective response, the window of opportunity would still be small. Given low awareness and even less direct action among developing nations' intellectuals, only a well-orchestrated, intentionally organized effort offers any success.

RECODIFICATION IN NON-WESTERN NATIONS

Working in these early days of power of a third kind, the primary strategic objective for non-Western countries will be to minimize the effect of any effort to separate politics from culture and the individual from creating his own political process.

If this single non-Western objective is not realized, the Western campaign for supra-national political status will necessarily create dysfunctional barriers between citizens and their indigenous cultures. Thus if the campaign is successful in its own trivialized terms, it could create even more turbulence in already stressed developing countries. This could end in doing more harm than good to the already discernible movement toward higher levels of citizen involvement.

Developing nations' intellectuals must confront that which is false: the assumption that Western culture's concept of Man, its definition of democracy and of human rights, is the only truly human standard for all political processes and choice. Rejecting concepts simply because they are Western will do little to make this false assumption transparent. If non-Western nations are to effectively confront a strategy of forced choices, they must go through the process of internal recodification[1] of concepts to harmonize with changing circumstances.

This recodification should not be done by adherence to the restrictive and intentionally ambiguous definitions of democracy and human rights currently projected by the West. At base, developing nations' intellectuals should be clear on this point: There should be a consensus of total disinterest in any promoted construction that, in thought or action, separates their politics from their histories and cultures. In the process of recodification, they should have the vision not only to explore for the hidden treasures within their own cultures, but they also should have the courage to admit their misinterpretations and abuses and to correct them.

Next, they should make a clarion call for transnational accountability. If developing nations' intellectuals want democracy, they should let everyone know that they do not want to participate in the dance of democracy. They should reject the artificiality of pointing to their most recent election validated by visiting Western elites or non-governmental organizations (NGOs). Nothing can be gained by allowing themselves to be the next site for yet another liberal democratic issue. Neither should they want to consider the adoption of "liberty" or "freedom" in Western terms either just before or just after a visit from the International Monetary Fund (IMF) or the World Bank.

Nations should make clear exactly what they do want. As a start, most peoples want the dignity gained by knowing that their hopes for their nation, the needs of their families, and their individual dreams for liberty and progress are considered important. When actions are taken that contradict these aspirations, they want clearly communicated justifications and remedial processes. Taken without all the emotional loading of Western-promoted doctrine, these are truly fundamental human rights. National recodification should be just as clear about how such rights are to be developed and protected within the cultural and institutional process by and for the individuals living within their own national borders.

The political desires of non-Western citizens are much easier to understand than the political inertia of their intellectual counterparts. Currently, many developing nations' intellectuals are much more respondent to Western blandishments meant to mobilize the acceptance of democracy. The role of the intellectual is to contest this orchestrated transnational discourse. If Western efforts go uncontested by developing nations' intellectuals, their inaction will ratify the appropriateness of the tenets of this global campaign. By standing aside, their acquiescence grants legitimacy to the claim that their indigenous culture needs to be set aside for the trendy Western one.

To forestall a Western inundation of currently divergent political processes, developing nations' intellectuals must move from receptors to actively involved communicators. They must dispense with the comfort of their current status-filled positions and petty perks like access to conference lounge chit-chat. They must stand in favor of processes that involve active engagement with local and regional issues rather than ritualistic affirmations of airy global universals. Political and social systems must be encouraged to evolve toward citizen involvement within the context of their indigenous history and culture—a type of evolution that could outlive transitory global symbolic gyrations.

Political dancing on a global stage of high-flying symbols, hyped-up conferences, and media transparency does not grant dignity to individuals working and living in their own local environments. Such orchestrated events are vehicles meant to persuade through shame rather than motivate through respect, to coerce by threatening exclusion rather than offering a promise of meaningful participation. Developing countries have not completely recovered from over fifty years of the "West versus the Evil Empire." They do not need another half-century of the West as valiant fighters against non-democratic forces, especially when such efforts are so often made to accomplish political and economic objectives.

Developing nations' citizens harbor more concrete political aspirations. They simply want freedom of expression and accountability. They want to see a clear continuity between the political processes and decisions that govern and represent their nation, their unique national history, and the national culture that has framed their choices and actions for centuries.

Recodification is not simply a good thing in and of itself. In this exciting period of change, there is real advantage in making the values and understandings of non-Western nations a viable part of a truly global culture. Attacking democracy and human rights as Western evils is yelling against the howling gale of change. In this non-insular world, higher levels of participation by all citizens is an unassailable value and an incontrovertible fact of the twenty-first century.

FROM THINGS TO THINKING

Non-Western nations' concept of Man must grant the primacy of thinking as an act, an act as available to human reflectivity as the lifting of a chair. In effect, their concept of human power must be stripped of the Enlightenment attack on subjective knowing and individual action. Non-Western thought need not cage human power into an ineluctable future of choices defined by Western liberal individualism.

When the driving force of the international effort to control change is understood as a project committed to the creation of a universal narrative, the analysis becomes clear. The true dividing line of power in the twenty-first century will be the sharp division between those who think only within and in terms of their immediate world, and those who think about how people in their own and in other cultures think about and react to every aspect of the entire world.

In these days of "spaceless" access to an absent global audience, pre-critical elites will be more vulnerable to manipulation and control. Meanwhile, their more sophisticated Western counterparts will become ever more effective in mobilizing meaning in search of exceptionality. Pre-critical non-Western elites will be pushed back and forth in a game of coercion or manipulation reminiscent of the Cold War. Reflective elites will have left that field to the already powerless, controlling the parameters of conflicts and cooperation well into the middle of the twenty-first century. This will require a truly remarkable effort on the part of developing nations' intellectuals to alter their assumption about the source of change and power. They have been trained to see the technology of "things" as the major source of change and the accumulation of capital and physical resources as the main source of power. Exclusive concentration on "things" must be altered to include a newly critical effort bent toward understanding the power of "thinking about thinking" itself. Once convinced that the electronically enhanced construction of the global story is an understandable way of reaching for power, they can begin to respond effectively to power of a third kind. Such a response could result in a strategy of reflective thought truly equal to this newly emerging arena of conflict.

Such a response can happen even as non-Western nations shore up the overwhelming demands of their peoples' struggle with scarcity. However, this will require a change of mind to meet unprecedented Western attempts to limit the powers of mind and action with narrow political constructs and agendas. Developing nations' intellectuals must revisit the pervasive assumption of Western divisions between intellectual thought and common sense, and between the educated thinker and the informally educated person. With the assumption that insularity is forever a part of an irretrievable past, they will grant a new importance to the common discourse of people in every level of life.

What they say and think about their world and the nature of the process of discourse in which they communicate and reflect is, more than ever, a prime force in intentionally and unintentionally created change.

Mediating Between the Past and the Future

It is ironic that Western intellectuals are now interested in reflective, critical thought. The West has locked Man into a supposedly ineluctable future where reflective thought can only elaborate on an already known and supposedly scientifically proven pattern. On the other hand, developing nations' intellectuals have locked themselves out of participating in the creation of the future by assuming that all the answers lie in the past. One functions out of a straightjacket created for the future, the other one is constrained by an assumption that the past is always present with answers for the future. Both approaches undermine the incredible potential inherent in human consciousness, reflective imagination, and interpretation. Both involve the trivialization of power and a politics of denial. Both are strategies filled with a kind of counterpower visited on those who deny the exciting and unyielding inconclusive nature of change.

The changes brought on by power of a third kind require that non-Western elites become educated in the ways that symbols are mobilized into vehicles of power. Man learned to use and to cope with every invention, from the sword to the microcomputer. Why not expand on the incredible potential of global uses of human subjectivity? Why not give culture-enriched politics the meaning demanded by the conditions of the twenty-first century?

Non-Western intellectuals must become critically aware of their own mental frameworks and the narratives that fill their discourse, shape their intentions, and inform their reactions. They must activate a "sixth sense" for how their own people frame choices, including the transgressions of individual and national sovereignty. With Daniel Yankelovich and other pollsters like him taking up residence so near the seats and halls of Western power, how can non-Western nations compete without an intentionally sophisticated technological and technical counterpart? They cannot afford to assume that this Western technical capacity will fail with people of their own nations just because they are so unsuccessful themselves.

Developing nations' intellectuals must become aware of the power of their own frames and narratives beyond the mundane function of being comforting cultural curiosities. Simply because these stories have been placed on the shelf does not mean that they are dead; it does not mean they are alive either. These narratives and the collective memory they comprehend are, like the language used to communicate them, alive only when they are actually used to represent the ways indigenous peoples make sense of their world. They gain strength only when they successfully pass test after test in the school of change.

On its own and seen in its proper context, such collective memory is a rich storehouse of experience. They are not merely stories; nor are they time-resistant answers. They should affect but not control the way this sharply changing world of today is valued and viewed. Intellectuals cannot be upset when their cultures are called traditional when, on the other hand, they refuse to recognize that change requires that *they* change the way they interpret the world.

The Power and Counterpower of Education

Developing nations' intellectuals must form an agenda for action focused on creating an educated critical dialogue, a dialogue that goes beyond defense to actually amplifying the inherent power of human thought. If they simply step aside in favor of inaction, energized intentional change goes forward, sparked by human exertions of power. In this, the dim light before the full brilliance of power of a third kind, the temporary comfort of inaction will be purchased at the expense of the future. If inaction is the mode of choice among developing nations' intellectuals, the next generations will literally consume—in and out of school—the projected expectations, values, and identities of political systems affording little continuity with their own culture.

This is a dangerous moment for non-Western intellectuals to approach education as a kind of follow-on from their roles as spectators in global affairs. Non-involvement in their roles as elite representatives of their countries' international relations is reflected in their roles at home as parents and citizens. They repeat current event dramatizations to each other in a kind of cant over petty domestic, commercial, or government problems. Their roles in nearly all official and unofficial identities become just that, roles. Only rarely do they seem to question the process of choice in their own lives.

In this context, education simulates the ineffectual chatting of their everyday discourse. It is not conceptually connected with a need to cope with unprecedented change. In the case of their children, education is "something they should have" or "something they have to get through." Again, they do not ask for the rationale behind such a casual analysis. Education should be a site for social and mental growth. But how much of either can they expect if the process of inquiry within both public and private institutions, including the family, is only different in terms of subject matter?

Education is necessary for preparing children to compete in a world that, for them, will always be a present world. They will act out of a "present" guaranteed to be dramatically different from the "present" found so challenging today. They will wake up in the morning faced with all the same fears and hopes of their parents but with substantially different problems and problem-filled scenarios. Who has the answers now for the problems they will have in the future? Today's parents and teachers can only train them to reflect critically on what they experience in their own time. Education must teach history as a source not as a solution. Historical text and context is important as a background for understanding current happenings. History is not sufficient nor equal to tasks that require a critical understanding and interpretation of events and change in the present.

Math and science and language are process skills involving critical thought but not necessarily teaching the ability to think critically. They are essential tools for understanding the shape but not the meaning of a situation. There is a need to commit to the assumption that the most important part of education is the intentional improvement of the process of critical thinking. People everywhere must move from a single-minded emphasis on *what* children should think to *how* they *think about thinking*. If they, like so many of us, question even the idea that international narratives could actually be intentionally formulated and used for global hegemony, they will be even more out of date than their parents and teachers.

Such education in critical thinking will teach our children how to cope with attractively presented fads of Western culture and the appeals to the supposed universality of Western political individualism. They will learn that the only route to individuality is the thinking individual. They will learn to analyze democracy, not to love or hate it. They will learn the advantages and disadvantages of democracy and free markets. They will learn that there is no magic more powerful or more healthy than the thinking individual in continuous interaction with his society.

The idea of education by dialogue is to learn to recognize the concepts introduced through power of a third kind and to either accept or reject the assumptions carried by Western narratives. Trained in critical thinking, our children can work effectively in the never-ending present, with all its contemporary pressures, while they inductively work their way toward answers to problems that impinge on the futures of their families.

COMING TO TERMS WITH POWER OF A THIRD KIND

There is no way out of this logic: The subjective self can only respond effectively to intentional intrusions by power of a third kind when the self is practiced in criticizing and intruding on his own thought. Because the individual self has become a *global* project, that effort can only be successful when the self is treated critically as a *local* project, allowing the individual to be both continuous and discontinuous with his culture. All of this is meant to say that the successful protection and projection of indigenous values and assumptions comes from the ability to critically evaluate them. Competing in an increasingly complex world demands skill in interpreting and conceptualizing that world and one's self in understandable terms. Trying to censor that world is part of the same counterproductive process that depends entirely on history and personalities for solutions. Active mediation between indigenous citizens of non-Western nations and the outside world is the only way of confronting a world that, today, is always inside as a globally pervasive process.

Critical thought derives from the source of human power. The commitment of developing nations' intellectuals to an intentionally energized process of critical thought results in a sense of ownership by citizens. Relying on censorship alone distorts meaning that the self gives to situations. In a non-insular world, training individuals in critical thinking is the best preparation for the future, an effort that is so much less risky than depending on a culture of monologue.

In this kind of dynamic atmosphere, all concepts are open to critical thought. They are out there, mutable and subject to discussion no matter how much they resonate with or contradict history. Discussion is enriched with arguments based on inductive reasoning, evidence, and intuition. Premises are of value when they are forced to stand on their own no matter who may or may not affirm them. In the end, the political system that will be more humane is the system most able to fully embrace this process of critical thinking. Education, properly conceived, encourages the capacities of consciousness, whereas propaganda does everything possible to constrain those capacities.

Power of a third kind is here. Its use in an agenda for gaining exceptionality is already in the initial activation stages by Western nations. But this agenda clearly overreaches those few countries currently capable of using it. Like all exertions of power, its incipient counterpower is already evident. The key to the use, the abuse, and the intrinsic vulnerability of this newly emerging power lies in the fundamental effect that will separate this age from those before it: transparency occurring as a result of electronic access to the sensibilities of nearly the entire human race.

The success or failure of this campaign has long-term implications for developed and developing countries. Again, the results are as two-sided as transparency itself. The campaign will use global awareness of turbulence to justify the granting of transnational exceptionality to the West as protector and judge of democracy, human rights, and free markets. However, because it requires the creation of distance between culture and politics, its success will certainly bring more turbulence in its wake. This campaign has already begun to evolve a grammar of ongoing conflict. This happens because it trivializes the power of *individual Man as he is* under the guise of expanding the freedoms of individualism based on *what Man ought to be*. It distorts the relationship between culture and politics and expands on Western democracy to the extent of making it a fetish. It takes an individual nation's choices out of its hands and places them inside Western ethnocentric constructs.

If developing nations' intellectuals continue to pursue a policy of uncritical non-participation, the counterpower built into this conflictual syntax will be the heritage of generations of citizens. If, however, the impact of this campaign and the emergence of power of a third kind is understood, the inherently false assumptions about human power, human culture, and human politics can be undermined.

The juggernaut of Western governmental, intergovernmental, and non-governmental forces are arrayed to push global universals from within an awesome edifice of systematized coalescence. This aggregation of ideological power will only increase as long as non-Western nations operate *within* the process created by the Western nations.

The agenda for the short term is clear: the conceptual creation of a multicultural international milieu where divergent systems are promoted rather than demeaned; where developing countries' education in critical dialogue allows them to establish their own interpretative frames and narratives; and where developing nations' intellectuals are actively involved in intensive, alternative discourse.

The game has begun. The ball is in the court of developing nations' elites. They can choose to play or they can stay in the stands and let the game be played with an entirely predictable winner and a just as predictable loser.

This is a pivotal moment for non-Western nations. It is a moment when the power to alter the course of human events is, as it always has been, in the minds of critical human beings.

NOTE

1. See Mohamad Aabed Al-Jabiri, *An Opinion on the Reconstruction of Modern Arab Thought* (in Arabic), (Beirut: Markaz Derasat Al-Wehdah Al-Arabeya, 1992), pp. 172–200.

Bibliography

Adams, Richard N. *Crucifixion by Power.* Austin: University of Texas Press, 1973.

Agnew, John, and Stuart Corbridge. *Mastering Space: Hegemony, Territory and International Political Economy.* London: Routledge, 1995.

Albright, Madeleine. *CNN WorldNews.* Cable News Network, 23 February 1997.

Alterman, Eric. "A Democratic Foreign Policy." *World Policy Journal* 13 (Summer 1996): 23–36.

Annan, Kofi. *CNN WorldNews.* 1996.

Appadurai, Arjun. "Disjuncture and Difference in the Global Cultural Economy." In *Global Culture: Nationalism, Globalization and Modernity*, edited by Mike Featherstone. A Theory, Culture & Society Special Issue. London: SAGE Publications, 1990.

Arat, Zehra F. *Democracy and Human Rights in Developing Countries.* Boulder, Colo.: Lynne Rienner, 1991.

Arnason, Johann P. "Nationalism, Globalization and Modernity." In *Global Culture: Nationalism, Globalization and Modernity*, edited by Mike Featherstone. A Theory, Culture & Society Special Issue. London: SAGE Publications, 1990.

Aron, Raymond, ed. *World Technology and Human Destiny.* Ann Arbor: The University of Michigan Press, 1963.

Atlanta Journal, Atlanta Constitution, Atlanta Journal and Atlanta Constitution, 4 May 1994–5 March 1995.

Augelli, Enrico, and Craig Murphy. *America's Quest for Supremacy and the Third World: A Gramscian Analysis*. London: Pinter Publishers, 1988.

Barnet, Richard J., and John Cavanagh. *Global Dreams: Imperial Corporations and the New World Order*. New York: Simon & Schuster, 1994.

Barnet, Richard J., and John Cavanagh. "A Global New Deal." In *Beyond Bretton Woods: Alternatives to the Global Economic Order*, edited by John Cavanagh, Daphne Wysham, and Marcos Arruda. Transnational Institute Series. London: Pluto Press with the Institute for Policy Studies and the Transnational Institute (TNI), 1994.

Bauman, Zygmunt. *Legislators and Interpreters: On Modernity, Post-Modernity and Intellectuals*. Ithaca, N.Y.: Cornell University Press, 1987.

Beck, Ulrich, Anthony Giddens, and Scott Lash. *Reflexive Modernization*. Stanford, Calif.: Stanford University Press, 1994.

Bell, Daniel. "The End of Ideology in the West." In *The Intellectuals*, edited by George de Huezar. Glencoe, IL: The Free Press of Glencoe, 1960.

Bell, Daniel. "The New Class: A Muddled Concept." In *The New Class?*, edited by B. Bruce-Briggs. New Brunswick, N.J.: Transaction Books, 1979.

Bell, Daniel. "Notes on the Post-Industrial Society." In *Power in Societies*, edited by Marvin E. Olsen. New York: MacMillan Publishing Co., 1970.

Bennett, Tony. "Media, 'Reality', Signification." In *Culture, Society and the Media*, edited by Michael Gurevitch, Tony Bennett, James Curran, and Janet Woollacott. London: Methuen, 1982.

Berger, Peter L. *Facing up to Modernity*. New York: Basic Books, Inc., 1976.

Berger, Peter L., Brigitte Berger, and Hansfried Keliner. *The Homeless Mind*. New York: Vintage Books, 1974.

Berger, Peter L., and Thomas Luckmann. *The Social Construction of Reality*. New York: Doubleday, 1967.

Bergsten, C. Fred. "The World Economy After the Cold War." *Foreign Affairs* 69 (Summer 1990): 96–112.

Billig, Michael. *Ideology and Opinions: Studies in Rhetorical Psychology*. Loughborough Studies in Communication and Discourse. London: SAGE Publications, 1991.

Boston Globe, 21 November 1993–12 December 1995.

Boutros-Ghali, Boutros. Foreword. In *NGOs, the UN, and Global Governance*, edited by Thomas G. Weiss and Leon Gordenker. Emerging Global Issues series. Boulder, Colo.: Lynne Rienner, 1996.

Bowen, Ezra. "The Posse Stops a 'Softie.' " *Time* (11 May 1987): 76–77.

Brands, H. W. *The Devil We Knew: Americans and the Cold War.* New York: Oxford University Press, 1993.

Brightman, Robert. "Forget Culture: Replacement, Transcendence, Relexification." *Cultural Anthropology* 10 (November 1995): 509–46.

Brown, James A. *Television "Critical Viewing Skills" Education: Major Media Literacy Projects in the United States and Selected Countries.* Hillsdale, N.J.: Lawrence Erlbaum Associates, Publishers, 1991.

Brzezinski, Zbigniew. "America in the Technetronic Age." *Encounter* 30 (January 1968): 16–26.

Carey, James W. "McLuhan and Mumford: The Roots of Modern Media Analysis." *Journal of Communication* 31 (Summer 1981): 162–78.

Chicago Tribune, 26 February–12 September 1995.

Chomsky, Noam. *Deterring Democracy.* New York: Farrar, Straus and Giroux, 1992.

Chomsky, Noam. "Objectivity and Liberal Scholarship." In *Power and Consciousness,* edited by Conor Cruise O'Brien and William Dean Vanech. London: University of London Press, 1969.

Christian Science Monitor, 29 September 1993–25 May 1995.

Christopher, Warren. "Clinton's Foreign Policy: Internationalism, Not Isolationism." *Current* 374 (July/August 1995): 16–25. Originally published as "America's Leadership, America's Opportunity," *Foreign Policy* (Spring 1995): 6–27.

Claude, Inis L., Jr. *Power and International Relations.* New York: Random House, 1962.

Clegg, Stewart R. "Narrative, Power, and Social Theory." In *Narrative and Social Control: Critical Perspectives,* edited by Dennis K. Mumby. Sage Annual Reviews of Communication Research, vol. 21. Newbury Park, Calif.: SAGE Publications, 1993.

Clinton, William. "President's Appearance on CNN's 'Global Forum with President Clinton,' Atlanta, May 3, 1994." *Foreign Policy Bulletin* 5 (July/August 1994): 5–15.

Clinton, William. "President Clinton's Speech at American University, February 26, 1993." *Foreign Policy Bulletin* 3 (May/June 1993): 2–7.

Clinton, William. "President Clinton's Speech to French National Assembly, Paris, June 7, 1994." *Foreign Policy Bulletin* 5 (July/August 1994): 2–5.

CNN WorldNews. 24 May 1996.

Cohen, Anthony P. *Self-Consciousness: An Alternative Anthropology of Identity.* New York: Routledge, 1994.

Collins, Richard. *Culture, Communication, and National Identity: The Case of Canadian Television.* Toronto, Ont.: University of Toronto Press, 1990.

Connaughton, Richard. *Military Intervention in the 1990s: A New Logic of War*. Operational Level of War series. London: Routledge, 1992.

Cooper, Barry. *Sins of Omission: Shaping the News at CBC TV*. Toronto, Ont.: University of Toronto Press, 1994.

Dahl, Robert A. "The Concept of Power." In *Political Power: A Reader in Theory and Research*, edited by Roderick Bell, David Edwards, and R. Harrison Wagner. New York: Free Press, 1969.

Dalby, Simon. *Creating the Second Cold War: The Discourse of Politics*. London: Pinter Publishers; New York: Guilford Publications, Inc., 1990.

Diamond, Larry. "The Globalization of Democracy." In *Global Transformation and the Third World*, edited by Robert O. Slater, Barry M. Schutz, and Steven R. Dorr. Boulder, Colo.: Lynne Rienner, 1993.

Dichter, Thomas W. Forward. In *The Road From Rio: Sustainable Development and the Nongovernmental Movement in the Third World*, by Julie Fisher. Westport, Conn.: Praeger, 1993.

Doherty, Carroll J. "New Drive to Overhaul Aid Faces Perennial Obstacle: Where the Clinton Administration Sees Reform, Congress Sees a Threat to Its Prerogatives." *Congressional Quarterly* 52 (15 January 1994): 74–76.

Edelman, Murray. *Politics as Symbolic Action*. New York: Academic Press, 1971.

Editorial. "Incorporating the World." *The Nation* (15–22 July 1996): 3.

Eisenstadt, S. N. "Intellectuals and Tradition." *Daedalus* 101 (Spring 1972): 1–20.

Ellis, Richard J. "Rival Visions of Equality in American Political Culture." *The Review of Politics* 54 (Spring 1992): 253–80.

Esquith, Stephen L. *Intimacy and Spectacle: Liberal Theory as Political Education*. Contestations Series. Ithaca, N.Y.: Cornell University Press, 1994.

Etzioni-Halevy, Eva. *The Knowledge Elite and the Failure of Prophecy*. London: George Allen & Unwin, 1985.

Falk, Richard. "Clinton Doctrine: The Free Marketeers." *The Progressive* 58 (January 1994): 18–20.

Farrar, Cynthia. *The Origins of Democratic Thinking: The Invention of Politics in Classical Athens*. Cambridge, England: Cambridge University Press, 1988.

Featherstone, Mike. Introduction. In *Global Culture: Nationalism, Globalization and Modernity*, edited by Mike Featherstone. A Theory, Culture & Society Special Issue. London: SAGE Publications, 1990.

Ferguson, Marjorie. "Invisible Divides: Communication and Identity in Canada and the U.S." *Journal of Communication* 43 (Spring 1993): 42–57.

Fernandez, Aloysius P. "NGOs in South Asia: People's Participation and Partnership." *World Development* 15 (Supplement 1987): 39–49.

Fisher, Julie. *The Road From Rio: Sustainable Development and the Nongovernmental Movement in the Third World*. Westport, Conn.: Praeger, 1993.

Foley, Michael. *American Politcal Ideas: Traditions and Usages*. Manchester, England: Manchester University Press, 1991.

Foley, Michael. "Progress." In *Ideas that Shape Politics*, edited by Michael Foley. Manchester, England: Manchester University Press, 1994.

Foote, Nelson N. "Identification as the Basis for a Theory of Motivation." *American Sociological Review* 16 (February 1951): 14–21.

Franck, Thomas M. "The Emerging Right to Democratic Governance" *The American Journal of International Law* 86 (January 1992): 46–91.

Freire, Paulo. "Cultural Action and Conscientization." *Harvard Educational Review* 40 (August 1970): 452–77.

Friedland, Lewis A. *Covering the World: International Television News Services*. Perspectives on the News Series. New York: Twentieth Century Fund, Inc., 1992.

Fukuyama, Francis. "Allies or Enemies? Confucianism and Democracy." *Current* 376 (October 1995): 15–21. First published as "Confucianism and Democracy" in *Journal of Democracy* (April 1995): 20–33.

Gaer, Felice D. "Reality Check: Human Rights NGOs Confront Governments at the UN." In *NGOs, the UN, and Global Governance*, edited by Thomas G. Weiss and Leon Gordenker. Emerging Global Issues series. Boulder, Colo.: Lynne Rienner, 1996.

Geertz, Clifford. The Interpretation of Cultures: Selected Essays. New York: Basic Books, 1973.

Geertz, Clifford. "On the Nature of Anthropological Understanding." *American Scientist* 63 (January/February 1975): 47–53.

Gerbner, George, Larry Gross, Michael Morgan, and Nancy Signorielli. "Charting the Mainstream: Television's Contributions to Political Orientations." *Journal of Communication* 32 (Spring 1982): 100–127.

Giaccardi, Chiara. "Television Advertising and the Representation of Social Reality: A Comparative Study." *Theory, Culture & Society* 12 (February 1995): 109–31.

Gillespie, Marie. *Television, Ethnicity and Cultural Change*. Comedia Series. London: Routledge, 1995.

Gillis, John R. Introduction. *Commemorations: the Politics of National Identity*, edited by John R. Gillis. Princeton, N.J.: Princeton University Press, 1994.

Gitlin, Todd. "Prime Time Ideology: The Hegemonic Process in Television Entertainment." In *Television: The Critical View*, edited by Horace Newcomb. 5th ed. New York: Oxford University Press, 1994.

Goldman, Steven E. "A Right of Intervention Based Upon Impaired Sovereignty." *World Affairs* 156 (Fall 1993): 124–29.

Gordenker, Leon, and Thomas G. Weiss. "Pluralizing Global Governance: Analytical Approaches and Dimensions." In *NGOs, the UN, and Global Governance*, edited by Thomas G. Weiss and Leon Gordenker. Emerging Global Issues Series. Boulder, Colo.: Lynne Rienner, 1996.

Gordon, David C. *Images of the West: Third World Perspectives*. Lanham, MD: Rowman & Littlefield Publishers, 1989.

Goshko, John M., and Thomas W. Lippman, "Foreign Aid Shift Sought By Clinton." *Washington Post*, 27 November 1993, sec. A, p. 1.

Greider, William. *Who Will Tell the People: The Betrayal of American Democracy*. New York: Simon & Schuster, 1992.

Grew, Raymond. "On the Prospect of Global History." In *Conceptualizing Global History*, edited by Bruce Mazlish and Ralph Buultjens. Boulder, Colo.: Westview Press, 1993.

Hall, Stuart. "Culture, the Media and the 'Ideological Effect.'" In *Mass Communication and Society*, edited by James Curran, Michael Gurevitch, and Janet Wollacott. Beverly Hills: SAGE Publications, 1982.

Hall, Stuart. "Our Mongrel Selves." *New Statesman & Society* 5 (19 June 1992): 6–8.

Hall, Stuart. "The Rediscovery of 'Ideology': Return of the Repressed in Media Studies." In *Culture, Society and Media*, edited by Michael Gurevitch, Tony Bennett, and Janet Woollacott. London: Methuen, 1982.

Halliday, Fred. *Rethinking International Relations*. Vancouver, B.C.: UBC Press, 1994.

Al-Hamad, Turki. "Is There Anything New in Political Thought?" (in Arabic). *Aalem Al-Fikr* (October–December 1996): 9–30.

Al-Hamad, Turki. "A World of Words" (in Arabic). *Al-Sharq Al-Awsat* (14 April 1996): 9.

Harries, Owen. "Triumphs Amidst Disaster: Clinton's Foreign Policy Success." *Current* 369 (January 1995): 12–18. Originally published as "My So-Called Foreign Policy," *The New Republic* (10 October 1994): 24–31.

Harvey, David. *The Condition of Postmodernity: An Enquiry Into the Origins of Cultural Change*. Oxford, England: Basil Blackwell, 1989.

Held, David. "Democracy and the New International Order." In *Cosmopolitan Democracy: An Agenda for a New World Order*, edited by Daniele Archibugi and David Held. Cambridge, England: Polity Press, 1995.

Held, David, ed. *Prospects for Democracy: North, South, East, West.* Stanford, Calif.: Stanford University Press, 1993.

Hinkelammert, Franz J. "Changes in the Relationships Between Third World Countries and First World Countries." In *Spirituality of the Third World: A Cry for Life: Papers and Reflections from the Third General Assembly of the Ecumenical Association of Third World Theologians, January, 1992, Nairobi, Kenya.* Maryknoll, N.Y.: Orbis Books, 1994.

Hippler, Jochen. "Democratisation of the Third World After the End of the Cold War." In *The Democratisation of Disempowerment: The Problem of Democracy in the Third World,* edited by Jochen Hippler. Transnational Institute Series. London: Pluto Press, 1995.

Hoagland, Jim. "Policy From the Top Down." *Washington Post,* 7 October 1993, sec. A, p. 23.

Hoynes, William. *Public Television For Sale: Media, the Market, and the Public Sphere.* Boulder, Colo.: Westview Press, 1994.

Human Rights Watch, American Civil Liberties Union. *Human Rights Violations in the United States: A Report on U.S. Compliance with The International Covenant on Civil and Political Rights.* New York: Human Rights Watch, American Civil Liberties Union, 1993.

Huntington, Samuel P. "Challenges Facing Democracy: What Cost Freedom?" *Current* 353 (June 1993): 22–27.

Huntington, Samuel P. "The Clash of Civilizations?" *Foreign Affairs* 72 (Summer 1993): 22–49.

Huntington, Samuel P. "Democracy and Armed Forces: Reforming Civil-Military Relations." *Current* 380 (February 1996): 17–21.

Huntington, Samuel P. *Political Order in Changing Societies.* New Haven, Conn.: Yale University Press, 1968.

Huntington, Samuel P. *The Third Wave: Democratization in the Late Twentieth Century.* Norman: University of Oklahoma Press, 1991.

Huntington, Samuel P. "The U.S.—Decline or Renewal?" *Foreign Affairs* 67 (Winter 1988/89): 76–96.

Huwaidi, Fahmi. "An Example of Islamic Co-Existence in the West" (in Arabic). *Al-Majallah* (13 July 1996): 34–35.

Ibn Khaldoun, Mokaddimat. *Writings of Ibn Khaldoun* (in Arabic). Edited by Drwish Al-Juwaidi. 2nd ed. Beirut: Sharif Al-Ansari Sons, 1995.

Imber, Mark F. *Environment, Security and UN Reform.* New York: St. Martin's Press, 1994.

Information Please Almanac. 49th ed. Boston: Houghton Mifflin Company, 1996.

Iyengar, Shanto. *Is Anyone Responsible? How Television Frames Political Issues.* Chicago: University of Chicago Press, 1991.

Iyengar, Shanto, and Adam Simon. "News Coverage of the Gulf Crisis and Public Opinion: A Study of Agenda-Setting, Priming, and Framing." In *Taken By Storm: The Media, Public Opinion, and U.S. Foreign Policy in the Gulf War,* edited by W. Lance Bennett and David L. Paletz. American Politics and Political Economy Series. Chicago: University of Chicago Press, 1994.

Al-Jabiri, Mohamad Aabed. *Democracy and Human Rights* (in Arabic). Beirut: Markaz Derasat Al-Wehdah Al-Arabeya, 1994.

Al-Jabiri, Mohamad Aabed. *An Opinion on the Reconstruction of Modern Arab Thought* (in Arabic). Beirut: Markaz Derasat Al-Wehdah Al-Arabeya, 1992.

Jacobson, David. Conclusion. In *Old Nations, New World: Conceptions of World Order,* edited by David Jacobson. Boulder, Colo.: Westview Press, 1994.

Jacobson, David. Introduction. In *Old Nations, New World: Conceptions of World Order,* edited by David Jacobson. Boulder, Colo.: Westview Press, 1994.

Jacoby, Tamar. "Reagan's Turnaround on Human Rights." *Foreign Affairs* 64 (Summer 1986): 1066–86.

Jhally, Sut. *The Codes of Advertising: Fetishism and the Political Economy of Meaning in the Consumer Society.* New York: St. Martin's Press, 1987.

Keech, William R. *Economic Politics: The Costs of Democracy.* New York: Cambridge University Press, 1995.

Kirschten, Dick. "Crisis Prevention." *National Journal* (11 December 1993): 2942–45.

Kissinger, Henry. "At Sea in a New World." *Newsweek* (6 June 1994): 36–38.

Kissinger, Henry. *Diplomacy.* New York: Simon & Schuster, 1994.

Kossok, Manfred. "From Universal History to Global History." In *Conceptualizing Global History,* edited by Bruce Mazlish and Ralph Buultjens. Boulder, Colo.: Westview Press, 1993.

Kotb, Sayed. *Social Justice in Islam.* Translated by John B. Hardie. New York: Octagon Books, 1980.

Krauthammer, Charles. "Intervention Lite: Foreign Policy by CNN." *Washington Post,* 18 February 1994, sec. A, p. 25.

Laakso, Liisa. "Whose Democracy? Which Democratisation?" In *The Democratisation of Disempowerment: The Problem of Democracy in the Third World,* edited by Jochen Hippler. Transnational Institute Series. London: Pluto Press, 1995.

Lake, Anthony. "Defining Missions, Setting Deadlines: Meeting New Security Challenges in the Post–Cold War World; Address to Students and Faculty at The George Washington University, Washington, D.C., March 6, 1996." In *U.S. Department of State Dispatch* 7 (18 March 1996) [database online]. Washington, D.C.: U.S. Department of State Bureau of Public Affairs [cited 3 July 1996, 13:12:10]. Available on the Internet from gopher@dosfan.lib.uic.edu.

Lake, Anthony. "The Four Pillars to Emerging 'Strategy of Enlargement.'" Excerpts from a speech given at the School of Advanced International Studies, Johns Hopkins University, Baltimore, Md., 22 September 1993. *Christian Science Monitor*, 29 September 1993, p. 19.

Lake, Anthony. "From Containment to Enlargement; Address at the School of Advanced International Studies, Johns Hopkins University, Washington, D.C., September 21, 1993." *U.S. Department of State Dispatch* 4 (27 September 1993): 658–64.

Lake, Anthony. "Press Briefing on the 'Presidential Decision Directive,' May 5, 1994." *Foreign Policy Bulletin* 5 (July/August 1994): 72–75.

Lake, Anthony. *Third World Radical Regimes: U.S. Policy Under Carter and Reagan*. Headline Series, no. 272. New York: Foreign Policy Association, January/February 1985.

Lasch, Christopher. *The Culture of Narcissism: American Life in an Age of Diminishing Expectations*. New York: W. W. Norton and Co., 1978.

Leps, Marie-Christine. "Empowerment Through Information: A Discursive Critique." *Cultural Critique* 31 (Fall 1995): 179–96.

Los Angeles Times, 17 December 1992–22 October 1995.

Magyar, Karl P. "Classifying the International Political Economy: A Third World Proto-theory." *Third World Quarterly* 16 (December 1995): 703–16.

Maynes, Charles William. "The New Pessimism: Wasn't the Cold War Better?" *Current* 378 (December 1995): 20–27. First published as "The New Pessimism" in *Foreign Policy* 100 (Fall 1995): 33–49.

Maynes, Charles William. "Relearning Intervention." *Foreign Policy* 98 (Spring 1995): 96–113.

Mazlish, Bruce. "An Introduction to Global History." In *Conceptualizing Global History*, edited by Bruce Mazlish and Ralph Buultjens. Boulder, Colo.: Westview Press, 1993.

McLuhan, Marshall. *Understanding Media: The Extensions of Man*. New York: Signet Books, 1964.

McLuhan, Marshall, and Bruce R. Powers. *The Global Village: Transformations in World Life and Media in the 21st Century*. New York: Oxford University Press, 1989.

Mehmet, Ozay. *Westernizing the Third World: The Eurocentricity of Economic Development Theories*. London: Routledge, 1995.

Menand III, Louis. "Human Rights as Global Imperative." In *Conceptualizing Global History*, edited by Bruce Mazlish and Ralph Buultjens. Boulder, Colo.: Westview Press, 1993.

Mernissi, Fatima. *Islam and Democracy: Fear of the Modern World.* Reading, Mass.: Addison-Wesley Publishing Co., 1992.

Miller, Marian A. L. "The Third World Agenda in Environmental Politics: From Stockholm to Rio." In *The Changing Political Economy of the Third World*, edited by Manochehr Dorraj. Boulder, Colo.: Lynne Rienner, 1995.

Mills, C. Wright. "Situated Actions and Vocabularies of Motive." *American Sociological Society* 5 (1940): 904–13.

Mills, C. Wright. *The Sociological Imagination.* New York: Oxford University Press, 1959.

Moores, Shaun. "Media, Modernity, and Lived Experience." *Journal of Communication Inquiry* 19 (Spring 1995): 5-19.

Morgenthau, Hans J. *Scientific Man vs. Power Politics.* Chicago: University of Chicago Press, 1974.

Morley, David. "Electronic Communities and Domestic Rituals: Cultural Consumption and the Production of European Cultural Identities." In *Media Cultures: Reappraising Transnational Media*, edited by Michael Skovmand and Kim Christian Schroder. Communication and Society Series. London: Routledge, 1992.

Murdock, Graham, and Peter Golding. "Information Poverty and Political Inequality: Citizenship in the Age of Privatized Communications." *Journal of Communication* 39 (Summer 1989): 180–95.

Natsios, Andrew S. "NGOs and the UN System in Complex Humanitarian Emergencies: Conflict or Cooperation?" In *NGOs, the UN, and Global Governance*, edited by Thomas G. Weiss and Leon Gordenker. Emerging Global Issues Series. Boulder, Colo.: Lynne Rienner, 1996.

Naylor, Thomas H. *The Cold War Legacy.* Lexington, Mass.: Lexington Books, 1991.

Nettl, J. P. "Ideas, Intellectuals, and Structures of Dissent." In *On Intellectuals*, edited by Philip Rieff. Garden City, N.Y.: Doubleday and Co., 1969.

Nettl, Peter. "Power and the Intellectuals." In *Power and Consciousness*, edited by Conor Cruise O'Brien and William Dean Vanech. London: University of London Press Ltd., 1969.

New York Times, 24 January 1993–11 April 1996.

Nisbet, Robert A. *Social Change and History.* New York: Oxford University Press, 1979.

Noland, Marcus. "Economic Cooperation in the Asia-Pacific: Openings for the U.S.?" In *Great Decisions*. New York: Foreign Policy Association, 1996.

Nye, Joseph S. Jr. *Bound To Lead: The Changing Nature of American Power.* New York: Harper Collins, Basic Books, 1990.

O'Brien, Conor Cruise. "Imagination and Politics." In *Power and Consciousness*, edited by Conor Cruise O'Brien and William Dean Vanech. London: University of London Press Ltd., 1969.

O'Brien, Conor Cruise. Introduction. In *Power and Consciousness*, edited by Conor Cruise O'Brien and William Dean Vanech. London: University of London Press Ltd., 1969.

O'Donnell, Victoria, and Garth S. Jowett. "Propaganda as a Form of Communication." In *Propaganda: A Pluralistic Perspective*, edited by Ted J. Smith III. Media and Society Series. New York: Praeger, 1989.

Olsen, Marvin E. "Power as a Social Process." In *Power In Societies*, edited by Marvin E. Olsen. New York: MacMillan Publishing Co., 1970.

Ong, Walter J. "World as View and World as Event." *American Anthropologist* 71 (August 1969): 634–47.

Parekh, Bhikhu. "The Cultural Particularity of Liberal Democracy." In *Prospects for Democracy: North, South, East, West*, edited by David Held. Stanford, Calif.: Stanford University Press, 1993.

Parsons, Talcott. "'The Intellectual': A Social Role Category." In *On Intellectuals: Theoretical Studies and Case Studies.* New York: Doubleday and Co., 1969.

Patel, I. G. "Global Economic Governance: Some Thoughts on Our Current Discontents." In *Global Governance: Ethics and Economics of the World Order*, edited by Meghnad Desai and Paul Redfern. London: Pinter, 1995.

Pinkney, Robert. *Democracy in the Third World.* Issues in Third World Politics. Boulder, Colo.: Lynne Rienner, 1994.

Plant, Raymond. "Rights, Rules and World Order." In *Global Governance: Ethics and Economics of the World Order*, edited by Meghnad Desai and Paul Redfern. London: Pinter, 1995.

Pogge, Thomas W. "Cosmopolitanism and Sovereignty." *Ethics* 103 (October 1992): 48–75.

Purdum, Todd S. "Clinton Warns of U.S. Retreat to Isolationism." *New York Times*, 7 October 1995, sec. A, p. 1, late edition.

Qualter, Terence H. *Advertising and Democracy in the Mass Age.* New York: St. Martin's Press, 1991.

Reid, Herbert G. Introduction to Part 1, "Mainstream Ideology as a System of Cultural Hegemony: Political Domination in Everyday Life." In *Up the Mainstream: A Critique of Ideology in American Politics and Everyday Life*, edited by Herbert G. Reid. New York: David McKay Company, Inc., 1974.

"Rio Declaration on Environment and Development, June 14, 1992." *Foreign Policy Bulletin* 3 (July/August 1992): 49.

Roach, Thomas. "Competing News Narratives, Consensus, and World Power." In *The U.S. Media and the Middle East: Image and Perception*, edited by Yahya R. Kamalipour. Contributions to the Study of Mass Media and Communications Number 46. Westport, Conn.: Greenwood Press, 1995.

Robbins, Bruce. Introduction. In *Intellectuals: Aesthetics, Politics and Academics*, edited by Bruce Robbins. Social Text Collective, Cultural Politics 2. Minneapolis: University of Minnesota Press, 1990.

Robinson, Gertrude Joch. "Mass Media and Ethnic Strife in Multi-National Yugoslavia." *Journalism Quarterly* 51 (Fall 1974): 490–97.

Robinson, William I. "Pushing Polyarchy: the U.S.–Cuba Case and the Third World." *Third World Quarterly* 16 (December 1995): 703–16.

Rodman, Peter W. *More Precious than Peace: The Cold War and the Struggle for the Third World*. New York: Charles Scribner's Sons, 1994.

Rosinski, Herbert. *Power and Human Destiny*. Edited by Richard P. Stebbins. London: Pall Mall Press, 1965.

Sagan, Eli. *The Honey and the Hemlock: Democracy and Paranoia in Ancient Athens and Modern America*. New York: Basic Books, 1991.

Sahin, Haluk, and Asu Aksoy. "Global Media and Cultural Identity in Turkey." *Journal of Communication* 43 (Spring 1993): 31–41.

Schattschneider, E. E. *The Semisovereign People: A Realist's View of Democracy in America*. New York: Holt, Rinehart and Winston, 1960.

Schiller, Herbert I. *Communication and Cultural Domination*. White Plains, N.Y.: M. E. Sharpe, 1976.

Schiller, Herbert I. "The Diplomacy of Cultural Domination and the Free Flow of Information." *Freedomways* 22 (Third Quarter 1982): 144–62.

Schiller, Herbert I. "The 'Information Highway': Public Way or Private Road." *The Nation* (12 July 1993): 64–66.

Schlesinger, James. "New Instabilities, New Priorities." *Foreign Policy* 85 (Winter 1991/92): 3–24.

Shabecoff, Philip. *A New Name for Peace: International Environmentalism, Sustainable Development, and Democracy*. Hanover, N.H.: University Press of New England, 1996.

Shils, Edward. *The Intellectuals and the Powers and Other Essays*. Chicago: University of Chicago Press, 1972.

Sikkink, Kathryn. "Human Rights, Principled Issue-Networks, and Sovereignty in Latin America." *International Organization* 47 (Summer 1993): 411–41.

Smillie, Ian. *The Alms Bazaar: Altruism Under Fire—Non-Profit Organizations and International Development.* London: IT Publications, 1995.

Snow, Donald M. *Distant Thunder: Third World Conflict and the New International Order.* New York: St. Martin's Press, 1993.

"Some Limits on the Global Village." *New York Times,* 4 May 1994, sec. A, p. 12, late New York edition.

Soroos, Marvin S. *Beyond Sovereignty: The Challenge of Global Policy.* Studies in International Relations. Columbia: University of South Carolina Press, 1989.

Spiro, Peter J. "New Global Communities: Nongovernmental Organizations in International Decision-Making Institutions." *The Washington Quarterly* 18 (Winter 1995): 45–56.

Steinbruner, John D. "Reluctant Strategic Realignment: The American Military After the Cold War." *Current* 372 (May 1995): 8–12. First published in *The Brookings Review* (Winter 1995): 5–9.

Stokes, Bruce. "The New Linkage." *National Journal,* 25 June 1994, 1509–14.

Stopford, Michael. "Locating the Balance: The United Nations and the New World Disorder." *Virginia Journal of International Law* 34 (Spring 1994): 685–99.

Suter, Keith. "How the Cold War Became an Expensive Irrelevance." In *Why the Cold War Ended: A Range of Interpretations,* edited by Ralph Summy and Michael E. Salla. Contributions in Political Science, no. 353. Westport, Conn.: Greenwood Press, 1995.

Talbott, Strobe. "Support for Democracy and the U.S. National Interest; Remarks Before the Carnegie Endowment for International Peace, Washington, D.C., March 1, 1996." In *U.S. Department of State Dispatch* 7 (18 March 1996) [database online]. Washington, D.C.: U.S. Department of State Bureau of Public Affairs [cited 3 July 1996, 13:12:10]. Available on the Internet: gopher@dosfan.lib.uic.edu

Tarabishi, George. *The Slaughter of Heritage in Modern Arab Thought* (in Arabic). Beirut: Dar Al-Sagi, 1993.

Tedstrom, John E. *Beyond Consolidation: U.S. Government International Broadcasting in the Post-Cold War Era.* Santa Monica, Calif.: RAND, 1994.

Tellis, Ashley J. "Terminating Intervention: Understanding Exit Strategy and U.S. Involvement in Intrastate Conflicts." *Studies in Conflict & Terrorism* 19 (1996): 117–51.

Thompson, John B. "Mass Communication and Modern Culture: Contribution to a Critical Theory of Ideology." *Sociology* 22 (August 1988): 359–83.

Twitchell, James B. "'And Now a Word From Our Sponsor.'" *The Wilson Quarterly* 20 (Summer 1996): 68–77.

"U.S. Fact Sheet: Agenda 21 Agreement." *Foreign Policy Bulletin* 3 (July/August 1992): 45–46.

U.S. House Committee on Foreign Affairs. *Oversight of the State Department's Country Reports on Human Rights Practices for 1993 and U.S. Human Rights Policy: Hearings before the Subcommittee on International Security, International Organizations and Human Rights of the Committee on Foreign Affairs.* 103rd Cong., 2nd sess., 1 February and 10 May 1994.

"U.S. Statement for the Record on Agenda 21 and the Authoritative Statement of Forest Principles, June 12, 1992." *Foreign Policy Bulletin* 3 (July/August 1992): 49.

Vernon, Raymond. "Seeds of Conflict: The Global Spread of Corporate Enterprise." *Harvard International Review* 17 (Summer 1995): 26–29.

Wall Street Journal, 6 April 1983–24 May 1996.

Washington Post, 15 November 1992–3 May 1996.

Weinstein, Jay. "The Third World and Developmentalism: Technology, Morality, and the Role of the Intellectual." In *The Mythmakers: Intellectuals and the Intelligentsia in Perspective*, edited by Raj P. Mohan. International Journal of Contemporary Sociology, Contributions in Sociology, Number 63. New York: Greenwood Press, 1987.

White, Robert A. "Mass Communication and Culture: Transition to a New Paradigm." *Journal of Communication* 33 (Summer 1983): 279–301.

Wiarda, Howard J. *Ethnocentrism in Foreign Policy: Can We Understand the Third World?* Washington, D.C.: American Enterprise Institute for Public Policy Research, 1985.

Williams, Daniel. "Clinton's National Security Advisor Outlines U.S. 'Strategy of Enlargement.'" *Washington Post,* 22 September 1993, sec. A, p. 16.

Wrong, Dennis H. *Power: Its Forms, Bases and Uses. Key Concepts in the Social Sciences.* New York: Harper and Row Publishers, 1979.

Yunis, Harvey. *Taming Democracy: Models of Political Rhetoric in Classical Athens.* Rhetoric & Society. Ithaca, N.Y.: Cornell University Press, 1996.

Zhang, Baohui. "Corporatism, Totalitarianism, and Transitions to Democracy." *Comparative Political Studies* 27 (April 1994): 108–36.

Index

About the Author

HISHAM M. NAZER is Chairman of the Nazer Group of Saudi Arabia. He has spent thirty-eight years in public service, twenty-eight as a cabinet minister. As Saudi Arabian Minister of Planning, he wrote the first five development plans of the Kingdom, guiding their implementation from 1970 onward. As Minister, he developed the concept for Saudi Arabia's two industrial cities, Jubail and Yanbu, directing their construction and management. From 1986 to 1995, Mr. Nazer served as the Minister of Petroleum, presiding over the restructuring and integrating of Saudi Arabia's oil industry, providing it with footholds in downstream operations in the United States, Korea, the Philippines, and Europe. At that time, he also served as the Chairman of Saudi Aramco, the largest oil company in the world.